M000011612

An American Soldier in World War I

An American
Soldier
IN WORLD WAR I

GEORGE BROWNE

EDITED BY DAVID L. SNEAD

University of Nebraska Press   *Lincoln & London*

Portions of this book previously appeared in
a slightly different form in the South Carolina
Historical Association *Proceedings* of 2003 and
are reprinted with the permission of the
South Carolina Historical Association.

Library of Congress Cataloging-in-Publication Data
Browne, George, b. 1894.
An American soldier in World War I /
George Browne; edited by David L. Snead.
p.   cm.—(Studies in war, society, and the military)
Includes bibliographical references and index.
ISBN-13: 978-0-8032-1351-7 (cloth: alk. paper)
ISBN-10: 0-8032-1351-4 (cloth: alk. paper)
ISBN-13: 978-0-8032-3281-5 (paper: alk.paper)
1. Brown, George, b. 1894—Correspondence.
2. United States. Army. Engineer Regiment, 117th.
3. World War, 1914–1918—Campaigns—France.
4. World War, 1914–1918—Personal narratives, American.
5. Military engineers—United States—Correspondence.
I. Snead, David L. (David Lindsey)   II. Title.   III. Series.
D570.31117th B76   2006
940.4'8173—dc22
2005025865

For Reagan, Delaney, and Darel

CONTENTS

LIST OF ILLUSTRATIONS

When I began this project in the late 1990s, I had little idea where it would lead or the number of people it would put me in contact with. It has been a truly rewarding experience, and I can only offer my deepest thanks to all who have touched this project at one time or another. The final product is much better because of their great help.

I began this study after Page Waugh, one of my students at Randolph-Macon College in Ashland, Virginia, offered to show me some letters that her great uncle, George "Brownie" Browne, wrote to her great aunt, Martha "Marty" Browne, during World War I. Neither Page nor I could have imagined at that moment what this chance encounter would produce. I am indebted to her for sharing the letters and introducing me to the rest of her family. Her father, John Waugh, and her aunt, Janet Hanson, are the closest living relatives of Brownie and Marty. They gave me permission to write a book based on the letters and offered extensive assistance in learning about Brownie and Marty's family history. Unfortunately, Lydia Waugh, Marty's sister, passed away during the early stages of my research, but she also provided important insight into her sister's life.

One of the joys of being a historian is meeting new and wonderful people at various archives, historical societies, and libraries. The staffs at the Connecticut Historical Society, the Connecticut State Library and Archives, the Francis Marion Library, the MacArthur Memorial Library and Archives, the Morris Historical Society, the National Archives of the United States, the Texas Tech University Library, the U.S. Army Military History Institute, the U.S. Military Academy Special Collections, the University of Nebraska–Lincoln Archives and Special Collections, and the Waterbury public library answered numerous inquiries and provided invaluable information. In particular, I would like to thank Mary Ellen Ducey, David Keogh, Bill Nelson, and Katherine Walter.

Numerous scholars provided guidance and support at various stages of this project. In particular, Pete Maslowski took me under his wing and constantly encouraged my efforts. While there may be no tougher critic, my book is better because of his advice. Many other friends and colleagues offered assistance, including Gretchen Adams, Alwyn Barr, Ernie Bolt, Jim Cooke, Bruce Daniels, Jorge Iber, Jim Reckner, and Don Walker. Several anonymous reviewers for the University of Nebraska Press also extended their invaluable expertise and insight.

The staff at the University of Nebraska Press has shepherded my manuscript with the utmost care. It has been my pleasure to work closely with Elizabeth Demers, Jeremy Hall, Beth Ina, Julie Van Pelt, and Chris Steinke.

I would also like to thank Randolph-Macon College and the University of Richmond for support in the early stages of this project. Additionally, Texas Tech University and the Big 12 Conference awarded me grants that permitted several research trips to Lincoln, Nebraska, Carlisle, Pennsylvania, and Washington DC. Without this, it would have been difficult to complete my research.

Finally and most importantly, I must thank my family. My mother, Marilyn Snead, offered unfailing support, and my brothers and sister provided many words of encouragement. My father and mother-in-law, D. C. and Carolyn Hughes, added to this project in more ways than they could imagine. I would have never been able to finish this book without the commitment of my wife, Lori, and children, Reagan, Delaney, and Darel. An unflinching supporter and one of my most careful critics, Lori has learned almost as much about Brownie and Marty as I have. As a wife, mother, and friend, there are none better. Reagan, Delaney, and Darel do not know how much they have meant to me. Whenever World War I became too consuming, I could always count on their love and desire for daddy time to force me to regain my perspective. They have truly blessed my life.

The United States declared war on the Central powers—
Germany, Austria-Hungary, and the Ottoman Empire—on
April 6, 1917, and joined a conflict that was already in its third
year. On that fateful day, Americans had to come to grips with
what this war meant and how it would affect their lives. George
E. Browne, or "Brownie" as he was better known, was a twenty-
three-year-old civil engineer in Waterbury, Connecticut, when
the United States declared war. [1] His girlfriend and soon to be
fiancée, Martha "Marty" Johnson, was nineteen years old and
a schoolteacher in her hometown of East Morris, Connecticut,
about fifteen miles from Waterbury. [2] Their lives, like many others, were forever changed by the war. [3] They endured a year and
a half of separation as Brownie served in the American Expeditionary Forces (AEF). They relied on their prewar memories
and an almost continuous exchange of letters to maintain their
relationship through this difficult time.

Little is known about Brownie and Marty before the war
started. It is unclear when they met and how their relationship
developed. The limited information that is available reveals,
however, a blossoming relationship in the summer of 1917 that
turned into a lifelong marriage after the war. Brownie enlisted in

the American army on July 8, 1917, and served in the AEF until February 1919. After enlisting, Brownie trained in the United States for more than three months before sailing to France in late October 1917. In France he prepared for combat while serving with the 42nd Division in a quiet sector of the front until June 1918. Starting in July and continuing through November, Brownie and the rest of his division participated actively in combat in the Champagne defensive, the Aisne-Marne offensive, the Saint-Mihiel offensive, and the Meuse-Argonne offensive.

Since Brownie and Marty did not see each other from October 1917 until his discharge in 1919, they wrote letters to keep in touch. While only a few of Marty's letters to Brownie survived the war, more than one hundred of his letters remain. His first letter was on July 8 and from that time forward, he wrote with great frequency while his unit was in training and as often as possible when he was in combat. His letters indicate that Marty wrote to him even more often. Brownie's letters offer a view of the experiences of an American soldier. He described the difficulties of training, transit to and within France, the dangers and excitement of combat, and the war's impact on relationships. While the letters reveal the war's strain on Brownie and Marty's relationship, their love never seemed to waver.

JULY 8, 1917 (Fort Slocum, New York)

Dear Martha:

I have often wondered under what circumstances my first letter to you would be written, but never dreamed of anything like this. I am now in the pay of the U.S. army—some pay.[4]

There were five in our bunch and we were all accepted after a three hour examination this morning. I thought the one in Waterbury was bad, but I found out something to-day.

We arrived here yesterday noon and spent most of the time until this morning in waiting for some-one or other. You should have seen the gang that came here with us. There are over 300 of them and I don't believe some of them ever had a bath. I don't want to give you a bad impression of the army though. They handle the crowd much better than I thought they would and the eats are pretty good considering the gang you have to eat with. Tomorrow we get our uniforms so then I expect to look the part. It will be better then anyway as we will be assigned to our company and our duties will be more regular. I will write you a long letter as soon as I get settled, and will be up to see you before we go into camp, if I can. . . . My address is Fort Slocum.[5] I wish I were spending next weekend at Bantam.[6]

Good-by my Martha and write soon to your own.

Brownie[7]

World War I began in late July and early August 1914 as European countries took up arms to settle long-standing disputes. The war had been brewing for a long time; many rivalries grew even more intense in the decades prior to 1914 over such issues as colonial territory, industrial competition, and military expansion. The assassination of Archduke Francis Ferdinand on June 28, 1914, sparked a crisis between Austria-Hungary and Serbia and ultimately led to a war between them starting at the end of July. Other states quickly became involved because of alliances between various European countries.[8] By the end of the first week in August 1914, the two warring sides had been drawn. The Central powers, composed of Germany, Austria-Hungary, and later the Ottoman Empire, clashed with the Triple Entente formed by Great Britain, France, and Russia. Italy subsequently joined the Entente in 1915, and these countries became the Allied forces. While the war maintained a certain degree of fluidity on the eastern front, the war on the western front in France quickly settled into a bloody stalemate of trench warfare where neither side could gain a distinct advantage. In these trenches, millions of soldiers from both sides died over the next four years.[9]

Woodrow Wilson was president of the United States when the war began. He was elected in 1912, not because he was a nationally known figure or because he had a distinctive agenda, but because the candidacies of Theodore Roosevelt and William Taft split the Republican Party vote. As president in 1913 and 1914, Wilson was much more concerned with domestic issues and problems in Mexico than with events in Europe; therefore, the rapid deterioration of the European situation in 1914 surprised both the president and the country. Overwhelmingly,

1. George Browne at Fort Slocum, New York, in August 1917.
Courtesy of Janet Hansen.

2. Martha Ingersoll Johnson in 1918. Courtesy of Janet Hansen.

3. The first page of Browne's first letter to Martha on July 8, 1917. Courtesy of Janet Hansen, John Waugh, and Page Waugh.

however, Americans saw the war as Europe's problem, and Wilson acted accordingly by declaring the United States neutral in early August.

The United States remained technically neutral from 1914 to April 1917 but gradually assumed a more pro-Allies position. Many events and issues contributed to this movement, including extensive cultural ties to Great Britain and France, the German sinking of the *Lusitania* passenger liner in May 1915, and fears of Germany acquiring hegemonic control over continental Europe. While many Americans favored the Central powers either because they were German Americans or were simply anti-British (like many Irish Americans), more were tied by their ancestries to Great Britain and France. Another issue leading to a more pro-Allies position was the growing economic ties between the Americans and the Triple Entente. Because of the British blockade against Germany, it was much easier for Americans to trade and bank with the Allied countries than with those of the Central powers. These growing economic ties gave many Americans a vested interest in an eventual Allied victory. A final factor influencing American neutrality was the effectiveness of British propaganda in depicting the Germans as barbarians.[10]

Despite these circumstances most Americans did not want to enter the war even at the beginning of 1917.[11] This mood changed, however, with a series of events in the first few months of that year. In January, the Germans reneged on the "*Sussex* pledge," which had kept Germany from attacking unarmed merchant vessels beginning in 1916. When Germany resumed its attacks in February 1917, President Wilson viewed it as a critical threat. The sinking of several neutral ships and the deaths of Americans in March highlighted the dangers of Germany's policy. Also, in February the Germans attempted to persuade Mexico to join it in an alliance against the United States. The German proposal, in the so-called Zimmermann Telegram, offered Mexico part of the territory it had lost in the Mexican-American War in exchange for joining the Central powers. The British intercepted and decoded the telegram and then provided it to the Wilson administration. Wilson ultimately released it to the American public, who reacted with outrage. These events, in combination with the aforementioned cultural and economic ties, led Wilson to ask for a declaration of war on April 2, 1917, and Congress voted its approval on April 6.[12]

The United States was woefully unprepared for the war despite almost three years of observing the fighting in Europe. The country's military establishment was small and undertrained, and its economy was far from mobilized for war. The United States had to expand the size of its forces dramatically and move its army to Europe in a very short time. This was not an easy task, and it took until the summer of 1918 before a significant American presence was felt on the battlefield. Timing was crucial: the Germans resumed submarine warfare believing they could defeat the British and the French before the Americans could tip the balance. Germany's gamble failed, and by the fall of 1918, the United States was supplying the necessary manpower to turn the war's tide.

Historians, journalists, and others have written numerous books describing American participation in the war.[13] Studies of the average American soldier, or "doughboy" as he was known, are also quite prevalent. Altogether almost four million men served in the army, and nearly two million of these spent time overseas. Although American doughboys served much shorter periods on the front than their Allied and enemy counterparts, they still experienced many of the same hardships, such as living in trenches and surviving lice, poor food, inadequate clothing, enemy bombardments, enemy attacks, and their own offensives. While the soldier's story has been told on occasion, most such studies fall short in several key areas.[14] First, they often do not provide the soldier's personal view. Second, they provide few, if any, citations for their examples and factual information. Students wanting to do more detailed research using primary sources would be hard pressed to find references in these works. This book overcomes some of these shortcomings by tracing one doughboy's experiences—George "Brownie" Browne—while placing them in the war's larger context.

Brownie's letters provide the organizational structure for each chapter. Individual letters, or sections from them, are followed by a documented explanation of their context. Letters are often grouped around specific themes or issues to provide more continuity to each chapter. These themed groupings detail Brownie's experience and what was happening in his small part of the

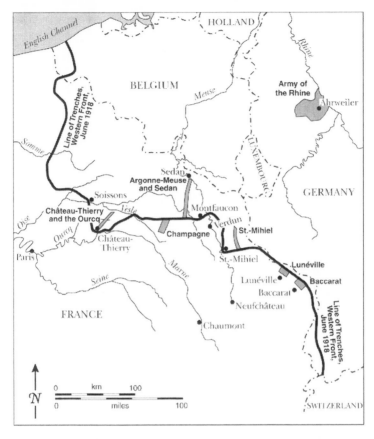

1. Areas where Browne served in France as part of the 42nd Division in 1918–19. *Source:* UNLA, RDC, RDVA, Box 18, Folder 7.

war. The letters are presented as they were written, including misspellings, grammatical errors, and slang from the time period. Reading the letters within the larger context of the war's events gives a window onto what Brownie—the average American doughboy—experienced in World War I.

ONE

Mobilization and Training
in the United States

When the United States declared war on Germany in April
1917, Brownie was working in Waterbury, Connecticut. As
his letters reveal, he enlisted for several reasons, not the least
being a sense of duty to his country and a desire to have a choice
in his assignment. [1] Enlistees had some choice in their assignments, while draftees did not. Brownie was officially processed
into the army in early July and was eventually assigned to the
117th Engineers Regiment, 42nd Division.

He immediately began writing letters to Marty describing the
process of becoming a soldier. His letters hint at some of the
time period's ethnic and racial attitudes, mention critical equipment and clothing shortages, discuss how the soldiers entertained themselves, indicate the importance of camaraderie, and
reveal the impact of separation on relationships. Other soldiers
experienced most of these issues and had their own interpreta-
tion of them. Brownie's letters capture the views of one soldier,
offering insight into his initial few months in the military and
America's efforts to build an army.

His experiences not only reveal the extraordinary evolution
of a soldier, but also a glimpse of his budding romance with
Marty. The war affected society in so many ways that it is difficult

for today's reader to recognize the immensity of the transition that the country and its citizens underwent. However, one must understand this transition and how the United States handled it in order appreciate the sacrifices Americans made in the war.

The American military faced an unprecedented task when the United States entered World War I. No one in the spring of 1917 knew exactly how large a contribution the United States would have to make to the Allied war effort. Raising an army was relatively easy. Many, like Brownie, flocked to enlist, while others were drafted under the provisions of the Selective Service Act of 1917. Much more difficult, however, was actually preparing the men for battle. From the lack of trained officers to shortages in housing, the military had a long way to go before it could become an effective fighting force. Brownie's enlistment and transformation into a soldier indicate some of the army's problems in making the transition from peacetime to a war footing.

JULY 9, 1917 (Fort Slocum, New York Harbor)

Dear Martha,

Over two days spent in this place now, and believe me it seems a year. We all have our uniforms now and are pretty *swell* looking soldiers? I don't think anyone would recognize us should we blow into Waterbury now. You never saw as much red tape as we have to go through here. It took us all day yesterday to get examined and sworn in and nearly all of to-day to get our uniforms. At that all they do is to look at a fellow, call out the size of some garment and another fellow throws it at you. The experience so far has certainly been worth a lot.

Am feeling rather "on the bum" to-day but am undecided as to whether it is caused by the grind or the treatment for typhoid. I will tell you about the examination in fact about the whole of yesterday so you can see how it is here.

We got up at five o'clock, (an everyday occurance) had breakfast at six. It was some meal. All right in quantity but I could not say that about the quality. First corn-flakes and milk and you know I like milk so took a lot. It didn't look much like Jersey milk and certainly did not taste like it. At first I thought we must be late & someone had put dish-water in the pail by mistake. I found out later that it was plain water with just enough condensed milk in it to make the right color. The rest of the breakfast was pretty good until we came to the *last course*, get that—two hard boiled eggs. They looked as if they had been picked up from under the roost. . . . However I never even cracked my two because Bayou (one of the fellows in our party) started on his first and I got a look at the inside. I don't know whether the egg was older than I am or not, but at any rate it was stronger than both Bayou and myself so we both started out. They call the eating house messroom and it certainly is an awful *mess*. For eating we have our mess-kits and they are a small canvas bag that contains everything we use to eat with. There is a knife, fork, spoon, cup and a sort of oval dish with a handle and cover—all aluminum. Well we left the mess room without losing our breakfast and went to wash up our dishes. There are just two long tanks full of water and heated by steam being forced into them. No cloths of any kind so we use newspapers to dry dishes.

About seven we lined up to go to the hospital. We must have arrived there about eight and had our numbers painted on our left hands. Mine was 56. First we signed two papers; (have forgotten what they were) next we had all the finger-prints of both hands taken. It made me feel like a criminal. At this point we had another wait of a half hour. Then there were questions galore more papers to sign. I don't know how many times I have told different ones how old I was when & where I was born, etc. Then the dentist took his turn. Then our eyes and ears. You would laugh to see the officers slam the men through. Most of the recruits were so scared that they couldn't see or hear anything anyway. Then we all filed into a dark hall-way to have our ears, nose and throat looked at. There was a surgeon sitting at one end with some sort of powerful reflector fastened above his left eye. I don't know where all the light came from but he could throw it where he wanted to look. He certainly was rough. Jab and something was in your throat then slam your head around and put something warm in your ears. He didn't even seem to be afraid of hurting *my* feelings. I believe he said "tonsils" when he looked at me. . . .

After waiting for about twenty minutes we were ordered out of doors and had to run about a quarter of a mile to another building. Here we stripped, hopped around the building twice; using first one foot then the other. Then two more doctors examined every remaining part, not forgetting anything. In this same building we were measured for our shoes. At last we were enlisted. They read the oath to you and all you have to do is raise your right hand and say, "I do!" I thought it was all over then but no. In still another building we [received] our typhoid immunization treatment, also were vaccinated. The treatment for typhoid is rotten and the worst of it is that there are two more of them coming. They paint a spot just in back of your right shoulder with iodine and you have to march in line up to a fellow with a big syringe. I suppose the worst part of it is seeing . . . others get it but they certainly give one an awful jab. My shoulder is sore yet but is much better. . . .

This morning we had drill for about three hours, raining more or less all of the time. Some job, the army. All were having pleasant dreams of spending the afternoon on our cots, but at roll-call this noon, two of our five were detailed for kitchen duty. Of course I was one of the two. That is supposed to be a hard job, but I was in the butcher shop all afternoon with nothing to do. About half of the fellows were shooting crap[s]. This army post is the worst place for gambling that I ever heard of. Our kitchen duty will get us out of bed before five in the morning as we have to report at five-twenty. We have no one to call us but failure to report means 30 days in the guard-house and a fine of two months pay. There is no such thing as an excuse here. If you are told to do a thing you have to do it, that is all, so I imagine I will be around at 5:20 a.m. tomorrow. If you should ask about how you were to wake up I imagine the corporal would tell you that he didn't care a damn or that you could sit-up all night. Our kitchen duty will be over tomorrow at 2 p.m., so I should[n't] worry. Then we are excused from drill in the morning so it is not so bad. I could write lots more to you but perhaps you will get sick of reading all of this. It is nearly nine so I must stop anyway. Write to me when you can Marty, for you know how much I think of you, and this is a good place to make a fellow think more than ever of his girl. As if that were possible for me. I am sure it isn't.

                                                                    Brownie

Brownie's experiences in these first few days of service were typical, as the United States simply was not ready to participate in the war. When Congress declared war, the regular army consisted of 127,588 officers and men, with an additional 5,523 men in the Philippine Scouts. Another 80,446 National Guardsmen were in federal service, mainly dealing with the Mexican crisis. In total size, the army ranked sixteenth in the world, right behind Portugal.[2] The army grew over the next year and a half to almost 3.7 million men.[3] To say the army was not prepared for the carnage of World War I is the greatest of understatements. Few Americans, inside or outside of the military, had any idea of what the combat on the western front in France was like. At most, there were a handful of veterans in the military who had gained combat experience in the Spanish-American War or chasing Pancho Villa in Mexico.[4] Neither one of these encounters was adequate for preparing men for trench warfare.

The declaration of war precipitated an economic and military mobilization unseen since the American Civil War. In ways it was more difficult, as for the first time in its history the United States had to transport a large force across the Atlantic Ocean to participate in a European war. Despite the war having started in 1914, the army general staff and, for that matter, President Wilson, failed to anticipate or plan for sending a large number of ground forces to Europe. This insufficient planning hampered the American war efforts until the end; the military never fully overcame organizational, supply, and transportation difficulties, but it had little choice but to face the daunting challenges before it.[5]

One of the initial questions President Wilson faced was who would command the American forces sent to France. Partisan political questions and other issues complicated the choice. The most prominent military figure in the country at the time, Maj. Gen. Leonard Wood, was unacceptable because he was tied to the president's political enemies, and he had a brain injury from the Spanish-American War. He also lacked recent field service. Wilson instead turned to John "Blackjack" Pershing, the most junior of the six major generals in 1917. Pershing had enjoyed a fairly illustrious career, including recent command of American forces in Mexico. Probably as important, he was known to be loyal to his civilian superiors.[6] The new AEF commander had the unenviable job of molding a fighting force basically from scratch.

Making matters even more difficult, the army had only enough housing in the United States for 124,000 soldiers in April 1917.

There were ten times that number just in the army by the end of the year. To accommodate this surge in manpower, the army constructed sixteen tent camps in the South and sixteen wooden cantonments in the North. Furthermore, it operated seventeen other training camps to provide specialized training in subjects ranging from engineering to the artillery. The construction of these camps illustrates how much the country had to do just to establish the bases to train the new soldiers. Each of the cantonments required twenty-five million board feet of lumber, seven thousand casks of nails, and numerous other building supplies.[7]

Expanding the military was relatively easy when compared to the logistical nightmare of training and equipping such a large force. The shortage of trained officers hampered all mobilization efforts. Altogether, there were only 11,000 officers in all the military branches in April 1917, and at least 200,000 were needed. In many cases, new officers stayed up late the night before learning the drills they were supposed to teach the recruits the next day.[8] Small inventories of weapons accompanied the shortages in manpower. For example, the army possessed only 600,000 Springfield rifles (model 1903) when it needed 2.5 million.[9]

The supply situation was also critical. The army constantly struggled to meet the needs of its expanding forces. Brownie's letters indicate that basic clothing and uniforms were in short supply. After almost three months, he still did not have a complete uniform. In 1917, the army had to order more than eighty million undershirts and underwear.[10] Supplying food also proved a prodigious task, as the doughboys ultimately consumed 800 million pounds of beef, one billion pounds of flour, and countless other quantities of items such as beans, bacon, coffee, and sugar. The army also had to provide certain luxury items such as cigarettes, of which it ultimately shipped twenty million a month to the soldiers.[11] While the army worked strenuously to provide supplies, shortages lasted to the end of the war.

JULY 12, 1917 (Fort Slocum)

My Own Marty,

We have our uniforms all right but I couldn't exactly call myself dolled up in it. They haven't even given us our coats yet; only one pair of shoes and one shirt. . . . We have two pairs of trousers, two changes of underwear, three pairs of socks and a hat. Some outfit, but we don't worry about anything.

SEPTEMBER 20, 1917 (Camp Alfred Mills on Long Island, N.Y.)[12]

We are all fixed up swell here now and quite at home. Yesterday we had a lot of stuff issued us. Even cots and bed-slips last night so we feel a little more civilized than before. There was plenty of straw to fill up the slips so we made some pretty good mattresses. I musn't omit to tell you what clothes I drew. A winter overcoat, olive drab cotton coat but no trousers, some socks and winter underwear. Expected to get the trousers to-day but they don't seem to be forthcoming. . . .

More news—I have just drawn another pair of shoes. Nice ones too—this is the third pair since I enlisted. We have a supply sargeant now so he looks after us some. He just told one of the fellows that our trousers would be in to-night and we'd get them tomorrow. Sounds good and I hope it's not a false report. . . .

Very much love from
Brownie

Immediately after the declaration of war, the War Department began to mobilize and issue calls for increased manpower. A variety of factors motivated young men to enlist.[13] One soldier recalled, "Like a lot of kids my age then [eighteen years old], I was looking for excitement and adventure. I thought this [enlisting] would fill the bill. It did."[14] Pvt. Martin Treptow of the 42nd Division's 168th Infantry Regiment carried a short saying in his pocket during the war indicating the sway of national pride: "America must win the war; I will sacrifice; I will endure; I will fight cheerfully and do my utmost; as if the whole struggle depended on me alone." He indeed did his utmost, as he later died on the battlefield.[15] A soldier from the 113th Engineers Regiment in the 38th Division remembered the influence of recruiting posters where "we could picture ourselves in the near future as pushing the Hun back from trench to trench, stopping only now and then to cut notches in the stocks of our rifles."[16] Other government propaganda reinforced these feelings. Newspaper headlines from the first day of draft registration read, "Manhood of Nation Will Register Today."[17] Sketches in newspapers showed mothers holding babies with the heading "What We're Fighting For."[18]

Although many men enlisted voluntarily, their numbers never met the military's manpower needs. Congress anticipated this problem and passed the Selective Service Act on May 18, 1917. In doing so, it deliberately avoided some of the problems arising from the draft during the Civil War by creating local boards to actually administer the inductions.[19] The government called all men between the ages of twenty-one and thirty to register by June 5, 1917. Each man was assigned a draft number from 1 to 10,500 at registration. On July 20, the War Department randomly selected draft numbers to organize the registrants into pools of potential soldiers. The men holding the first number selected went into the initial pool of available manpower, a process that allowed every registrant to know his likelihood of being called into service. The local draft boards were responsible for contacting any man assigned one of the first numbers selected and determining whether he should be inducted. Of those called for service in 1917 and 1918, two-thirds received exemptions or deferments due to physical defects, their occupations, marital status, or for other reasons. Altogether, the government registered more than 24 million men and ultimately inducted 2.8 million into the military.[20]

The pool of soldiers contained an interesting mix. Ultimately, the local draft boards inducted the men whose loss would least likely disrupt the home front. Many of the conscripts lacked formal education beyond sixth grade, fewer than 20 percent had high school diplomas, and less than 1 percent had a college degree.[21] Physically, they stood on average five feet, nine inches tall and weighed just over 141 pounds.[22] Brownie was actually bigger than most at five feet, eleven inches tall and 160 pounds.[23] The average age of all officers and enlisted men was just under twenty-five.[24]

The War Department divided the men into the regular army, the National Guard, and the national army, which was composed of draftees. However, the soldiers were ultimately mixed together and these distinctions were abolished in August 1918. Within the army, the division became the most significant unit. Due to shortages of equipment and trained officers, and the desire for staying power on the battlefield, the AEF organized divisions twice the size of those of its allies and enemies. At full strength, an American division consisted of 991 officers and 27,114 enlisted men. These men were subdivided into two brigades containing two infantry regiments each—approximately 16,000 men. The remaining men were dispersed among units ranging from the artillery brigade to the machine gun battalion to the engineers regiment.[25]

Although every unit was unique in certain ways, the case of Brownie's 42nd Division reveals some important issues concerning the training of soldiers and the development of new divisions. In early August 1917, Secretary of War Newton Baker directed "that a division of the National Guard composed of units which have the most efficient and best trained personnel, be selected from various States and organized for immediate service in France."[26] His true objective was to create a division around which the country could rally.[27] Soldiers from twenty-six states and the District of Columbia ultimately comprised the 42nd, or, as it was nicknamed, the Rainbow Division (see the appendix).[28]

The South Carolina contingent of the 42nd Division is of particular interest because Brownie was eventually assigned to the 117th Engineers Regiment, a unit that consisted of men primarily recruited from that state. In May 1917 the War Department requested that South Carolina governor Richard Manning organize engineering units that would be "ready for service in fifteen days."[29] The foundation for this request was the service of a National Guard unit of South Carolina engineers in Mexico the previous year. Governor Manning asked J. M. Johnson, the commander of the state's engineers, to recruit soldiers to fill his own unit, Company A based in Marion, and to create two new companies, B and C. Johnson established his headquarters for recruiting in Columbia and quickly established Company B there, while Company C organized in Spartanburg.[30]

All three South Carolina companies trained at their home bases in Columbia, Marion, and Spartanburg until mid-August when they came together for the first time at Camp Sevier in Greenville.[31] Each locality rallied around its company, especially the small town of Marion, whose newspaper clamored for support for the troops: "It will be the duty of all citizens," it exhorted, "to see that the men are entertained and comfortable while here. They are 'out there' in our defense, and within a short time will go to the front in France. Many will not return."[32]

The three companies stayed at Camp Sevier for less than two weeks before the War Department designated them the 1st Battalion, 117th Engineers Regiment, 42nd Division. Out of the 736 officers and men in the 1st Battalion, when it went north to New York for more training, approximately 500 were from South Carolina and the remainder were from North Carolina and Tennessee. In New York the 2nd Battalion, containing primarily engineers from California, joined the 1st Battalion to form the regiment. Brownie was assigned to the 1st Battalion at this point. Colonel William Kelly became commander of the 117th Engineers Regiment on September 3, 1917.[33]

The 117th Engineers and the rest of the 42nd Division came together at Camp Alfred L. Mills on Hempstead Plain on Long Island. The division completed its mobilization on September 13, with Maj. Gen. William A. Mann as its commander and Col. Douglas MacArthur serving as its chief of staff.[34] The division was housed in tents, with each company, numbering approximately 250 men, assigned to one side of a street. Generally, ten men bivouacked in each of the tents.[35] Each company was responsible for clearing the area assigned for its tents. One of the greatest difficulties was providing adequate clothing and bedding for all of the men. Shortages in this area continued to plague the division throughout its time in New York.[36]

SEPTEMBER 5, 1917 (Fort Slocum)

Dearest Marty,

. . . Today I applied for assignment to the 117th Engineers at Garden City L.I., but I expect no results.

SEPT. 7, 1917

At last it seems I'm going to leave Slocum. Now I'm wondering how often I'll be able to get a pass at my new destination. I'm to leave here tomorrow morning if nothing happens so have been thru all the red-tape necessary to such a step. Seems as if I've been standing in line all day. Have turned in all the government property I had[—]that is rifle, bedding, everything except my clothes and personal property. . . .

They say *here* that engineers are going to France right off but that doesn't make it so. . . . 117th Engineers I guess I told you . . .

SEPT. 9, 1917 (Camp Mills on Long Island, NY)

I didn't get a chance to write to you yesterday. We were moving nearly all day and the way things are here I think I ought to be excused on the plea of self-preservation. I sure am in the army now but I guess I'd better tell you about things as they happened. Sat. morning we got wet the first thing (naturally). Had another examination and finally got onto our boat about 9 a.m. . . .

Well we got on the Long Island R.R. at Long Island City and finally reached this place about three p.m. We took our lunch from Fort Slocum so were not quite starved out. It's about a mile from the station out here to our camp and we had a load to carry too.

I've never seen anything to equal this camp as there must be over twenty thousand men here and they are from all over the country. In back of us they come from Alabama and in front from California. . . . Our company is the only regular company in the regiment. [37] Seems like we're in the Rainbow Division of the National Guard. The papers say we're going to France and I guess we are going somewhere. At least I hope we are not in winter quarters here. Had to put up our tents last night got three blankets and slept on the ground. I was nearly frozen to death about six times last night. Got up in the night and put on all my clothes except my shoes but no use. It's ten times as cold here as in Fort Slocum and the ground is as hard as a rock. We ought to have cots but they don't seem to be forthcoming. Such is life in the army tho. I'd rather be here than in Slocum cause it's more like being a soldier even if there is no hot water & beds. . . . I'm trying to get a special assignment to do engineering work so wish me luck.

SEPT. 10, 1917

. . . The YMCA here is simply a tent and it's just about as cold in here as outside.[38] That's going some, too. I never saw such a place for cold weather. The camp here is on what they call "Hempstead Plains" and it's as flat as South Dakota. The wind blows all the time, usually a gale. Take these conditions combined with the fact we've had nothing issued to us except three blankets since our arrival and imagine the spirit of our detachment. Don't know of any remedy except waiting. At any rate they don't ask us to do anything so that helps some. Last night I doubled up with another guy in the tent so we had two blankets under us and four over us. At that I was cold some during the night.

. . . I've been watching the S.C. engineers at drill this afternoon but can't say I was very much impressed with their skill. They are about as good natured fellows as one would want to meet tho, and I sure love to hear them talk. Their officers are just the same [as] they are. Nothing like the discipline here [as] there was at Fort Slocum, but I don't call that a change for the better as I'd rather they'd be strict. Then you always know where you stand. Here the officers go all over and no one salutes them.

The troops continue to come in here night and day. Seems to me as if they must have nearly the whole division here by now. To look at the camp I'd say they had the whole army here. . . .

I don't really feel like writing to-day. Feel more like taking a bath, but I haven't the nerve to get under a cold shower in this wind. I'm going to take one soon tho, if I freeze to death.

WEDNESDAY, SEPT. 12, 1917

. . . At last we're off the ground. Three nights on the hard ground and I was nearly all in. Don't ever try it as the ground is darned hard and cold too this time of year. I have a good bedfellow and we must have nearly a bale of straw to sleep on. We put one blanket over the straw and the other five over us so manage to keep fairly warm. Two of the fellows out of eight are laid-up from sleeping on the damp ground, so I consider myself lucky. One guy had tonsilitis but they don't stick anybody who can walk into the hospital here.

SEPTEMBER 14, 1917

. . . There are eight of us in the tent and nearly everyone is a different nationality. We get along like pie tho. Chipped in and bought a lantern & a gallon of kero[sene]. There's no lights here at night except in the Y.M.[C.A.] and they are so crowded that one hasn't a chance to get in. . . .

I'll try to give you an idea of this place is like. There's one main street running straight across the plains (very flat here). On each side of the street they put up mess shacks about 75 feet apart and in back of those the rows of tents run at right angles to the street. Is that clear? There is a company in each row of tents. Suppose there's a certain way that these camps are always laid out but I'm not wise enough to explain thoroly.

SEPTEMBER 20, 1917

We are all fixed up swell here now and quite at home. Yesterday we had a lot of stuff issued us. Even cots and bed-slips last night so we feel a little more civilized than before. There was plenty of straw to fill up the slips so we made some pretty good mattresses. . . .

Company D of Cal. just came in from a hike in their heavy marching order and they sure look nice. I don't know whether we of Headquarters get rifles or not but I imagine so. I'll tell you how we are arranged here by companies. They run in alphabetical order: A, B, C, Headquarters, D, E, F. There is also a Sanitary Train and some Signal Corps. That's the whole 117th Regiment.

SEPTEMBER 25, 1917

. . . Now I have news for you. Good or bad I don't know. The less I know the more contented I am. I've been transferred to Co. A. of the same regiment so my address in changed accordingly. Just transferred this morning so I am unsettled again. This outfit is almost entirely South Carolina boys but I think I'll get along just as well with them as anybody. . . . There are twelve of us in this tent and we are some crowded. Perhaps will get more tents soon tho.

OCTOBER 16, 1917

. . . They sent everything away to-day except what we carry in our packs. We havn't drilled to-day except they showed us how to pitch our shelter tents this afternoon. This morning I had my life insured for two thousand dollars. Don't tell my mother tho—she might send me something (not) good to eat. We only pay 65 cents a month on a thousand dollars. It's pretty reasonable considering the risk or maybe that isn't great. . . .

I didn't tell you they took even our cots and only left us two blankets to keep warm with. They did have the grace to leave us our straw, so we'll manage to live on.

Goodnight Marty

Brownie

While instruction in the fundamental skills of soldiering was the most important need at Camp Mills, many, more basic issues had to be addressed first. Personal hygiene was a major concern of the high command, and understandably so. Many of the soldiers had grown up in rural areas and had never been exposed to certain diseases or received any vaccinations. In fact, a mumps epidemic swept through the camp in late September and early October. The average soldier received vaccines for typhoid, paratyphoid A and B, and smallpox.[39] These vaccines were deemed so important that the division commander ordered that the schedule of medical treatment "be adhered to, and nothing will be accepted as evidence of protection except properly prepared and authenticated record of such inoculation."[40] Even more basic, some men had to be instructed as to how often to bathe and change their clothes. The men were ordered to bathe at least twice a week and to change their underwear with at least the same frequency.[41] Finally, officers were made personally responsible for their men's sexual behavior. A general order requested,

> All officers serving with troops should do their utmost to encourage healthful exercises and physical recreation and to supply opportunities for cleanly social and interesting mental occupations for the men under their command; to take advantage of favorable opportunities to point out, particularly to the younger men, the inevitable misery and disaster which follow intemperance and loose living and that venereal disease which is almost sure to follow intercourse with loose women is always a serious matter.[42]

Brownie was fully cognizant of inoculations and medical examinations. The process began with his enlistment and continued through his stay at Camp Mills. Few things in his letters received as much condemnation as the shots.

JULY 29, 1917 (Fort Slocum)

My Martha,

. . . Am feeling very fit this a.m., except for my right arm. Received the third dose for typhoid last night, so that explains it. Nevertheless, the morale of the troops is excellent. . . . Am getting used to being punctured regularly, now that I am thru. The examinations never end tho, so we will be ready for anything soon.

AUGUST 6, 1917

. . . I didn't know but we'd be marched to the hospital for another inoculation. Seems there's another coming any day now. This is something new and is to immunize us against paratyphoid. I know what typhoid is but what is it with a para- in front of it? If there's any virtue in serums we ought never to be sick again.

SEPTEMBER 20, 1917 (Camp Mills)

. . . We didn't drill to-day. Yesterday was inoculation day and the whole gang is sick. This is my second dose here and I wish it were the last forever. You get very little sleep with an arm like mine. The dose is so much stronger here than in Slocum. Some of the guys have been in bed all day but the rest have been fixing the tent. We have a gravel floor now and a ditch all around the outside. Between getting clothes and inoculations our gang has had lots of rest this week.

SEPTEMBER 29, 1917

. . . So you think I'm mad at something. . . . Try to make allowances for your Sammie Marty.[43] Sometime it's harder to be near what I should be than at others. Now for instance my arm is as sore as the deuce or devil and that doesn't improve my temper much. We are done with the triple doses now. Honest you can't sleep the night after you get one. . . .

From your own,
Brownie

With the basic issues of hygiene addressed for the time being, the focus at Camp Mills fell to turning the men into soldiers. Army commanders had three specific training goals at the camp: discipline and unit cohesion; physical fitness; and basic drill movements and soldier duties. The general order for training stressed, "Discipline and physical fitness have never been more conspicuously essential in warfare than at the present time and upon these two cardinal qualities the education of the soldier must be founded."[44] A first lieutenant put it more bluntly: "The stay at Camp Mills was concerned chiefly with the hard work prepatory [sic] to crossing the ocean; equipping, packing and discarding; and not least of all, whipping the troops into shape."[45]

Training began early each day with reveille at 5:30 a.m. Sundays were the exception as soldiers were allowed to sleep until 6:30 a.m. After breakfast, the men drilled from 7:30 to 11:30, then broke for lunch until 1:15. They then participated in more drills until 4:30. Dinner was at 6:00, and taps was sounded at 9:45. The drill schedule was basically the same for four weeks except that the practice marches on Mondays and Fridays of each week were extended. The first week had marches of between five and six miles without packs or equipment. By the end of the fourth week, the soldiers were marching eight miles, fully equipped. Beyond marching, the soldiers' training included close order drills, instruction in their specific areas of expertise (such as infantry, artillery, or engineering), and basic first aid.[46] Soldiers were not trained, however, in trench warfare.[47]

The preparation the men received was limited. As the foremost historian and a veteran of the 42nd Division argues, because of shortages of equipment, this "period in which so much training could have been had, had the means been available, could only be devoted to elementary drills, close order drills, and reviews of the brigades and the Division."[48] One officer described it as a time "to prepare the fit and weed out the unfit."[49] Another significant problem was the officers' lack of training.

One young soldier recalled, "Our officers . . . were as green in the art of soldiering as we were."[50] The men found the drills challenging regardless of what the officers thought. Pvt. Rollyn Leonard wrote his sister claiming, "I get more out of a night's sleep on the hard ground than I ever did on a bed in Civil life. Some people imagine Army life nowadays is soft, but I wish they could see or indulge in a little of it, for we are getting worked now, the hardest kind of work there is."[51] Brownie provided the same type of descriptions of his experiences at Fort Slocum and then Camp Mills.

JULY 12, 1917 (Fort Slocum)

My Own Marty,

. . . Was up at 4:20 the a.m. We have to get up that early whenever there is a bunch of recruits leaving for their posts. There were 2200 in the bunch this a.m. It was some drill this morning. Drill lasts from 7:20 till 11, and they put you through some awful stunts. You ought to see some of the fat lads sweat.

JULY 15, 1917

. . . The days here are about the same. Usually rain and drill. They don't take us out if it rains hard but are not so particular about the sun. It is not monotonous in the least here. I like to drill and have had every afternoon but one to myself. It keeps one pretty busy to take care of himself and his outfit here. You have to shave and bathe, make your bunk, wash your clothes, shine your shoes. Then it uses up lots of time going back and forth to meals, to the post-office, to revilee at 5:30 a.m., roll-call at 1 p.m., retreat at 6:15 p.m. I wish you could see us stand retreat. The flag goes down and the band plays the Star Spangled Banner.

AUGUST 24, 1917

. . . They say that every smile adds a day to your life, but I won't fool the undertaker much by smiling to-night. Believe me I *am* tired. Only worked eight hours out of the last twenty-four but havn't had any sleep. The sentinels have to sleep in the guard-house and can't even take off their side-arms. If you had one smell of that place I don't think you'd sleep for a week. The prisoners are most of them dirty cusses I guess. We don't have to sleep with prisoners, of course, but right next to them. It's my opinion that the place is crumby (is that the correct spelling?) so I didn't sleep at all. . . . I'll never say again that they don't work you in the army. Yesterday morning five drills, getting ready and going on guard in the afternoon. Then I've had no time off to-day till now. See what I'm doing Marty and judge where my tho'ts are. Tomorrow a.m. five more drills and inspection at 11:15. This is *the* life! No clean clothes and my rifle rusty from the rain last night.

SEPT. 12, 1917 (Camp Mills)

. . . We have to drill about eight hours a day now and that combined with meals and other formations leaves me rather short of time to say nothing of sore feet and other small items.

SEPTEMBER 14, 1917

. . . Now I'll tell you my woes. I'm as tired as the deuce. Drilled all morning and had a five mile hike in the afternoon to-day. In fact we just finished the hike and the foot examination afterward. The last was worst. . . . The food is punk here too. Menu this a.m. One little slice of bacon, some rice, bread, and coffey without milk. Really all the meals are something like that. In spite of the hard work, bad meals and soft ground, I like it here. Wouldn't be surprised to find myself getting fat I'm so contented. I wouldn't go back to Slocum for anything. Really there is a sort of fascination about living here in tents. Perhaps I'll change my tune when it rains a few days.

OCTOBER 6, 1917

. . . The Lord only knows why they work us so hard here. I havn't had a minute to myself in the past three days till now and the rest of the regiment is in the same fix. Saturday morning we are supposed to have inspection and then be off till Sunday at 4 p.m. We had the inspection this a.m. all right and then another this p.m. just to keep us busy making up and unmaking our packs I presume. I never worked as hard in my life as I did yesterday. We had a practice march and engagement. Co. E. of this regiment were supposed to be the enemy. I was in the second line of advance guards on the left flank. We had to keep abreast of our company and watch for the enemy. Go thru back yards, orchards, gardens so we did fare pretty well. The great trouble was we were in heavy marching order and the heat was not to my liking. About three miles out we sighted the enemy and then the fun started. We have signals to advance and halt—no commands. We'd run a ways then fall down then up and run again. Imagine those heavy packs and rifles. At that it was lots of fun, but going back to camp we all nearly perished. Didn't get back till after five, all wet thru and tired out.

I don't know as they expect to use us as infantry in France. It's just the training everyone has to go thru. . . .

Good-bye my own sweetheart,
Brownie

A soldier's life was not all inoculations, drill, and work. Despite some of the hardships, Brownie and most of the other soldiers enjoyed the army. Soldiers loved receiving mail, played games when possible, and appreciated the camaraderie that existed in their units. Above everything, soldiers liked the passes allowing them to see loved ones or simply to get away from the camp. A member of the 117th Engineers described how "it was not all work and no play, for every now and then some of us were given leave to go to New York."[52] The men found twenty-four-hour passes fairly easy to obtain at least until the end of October; however, they did learn not to count on them. Leaves for longer than a day were more difficult to obtain and required headquarters' approval. If a soldier could not arrange a pass, visitors were generally allowed at the camp on Saturday afternoons and Sundays.[53]

While passes were relished, mail call was the highlight of each soldier's day. Brownie's letters show the immense satisfaction he felt from every piece of mail as well as the disappointment if none came. Beyond letters, soldiers sought amusement in a variety of ventures. Gambling was readily available especially around payday. There were normally nightly movies and vaudeville shows, and on most weekends, athletic events, including baseball and boxing. Magazines and newspapers were also available. On the troubling side, some of the amusements got out of hand and fights erupted between the white soldiers and blacks in New York, as well as between southern and northern whites.[54] Brownie, admittedly, was not immune to some of these prejudices.

JULY 12, 1917 (Fort Slocum)

My Own Marty,

I took a sneak down to the Post Office yesterday morning and got your letter. It certainly did me a world of good. . . . I like long letters, short letters, or cards, or anything you want to send me.

JULY 15, 1917

. . . There is always a ball-game going on here and usually two or three. Sat. afternoon is always a big time. Foot-racing and all sorts of athletic events. Last night there were three boxing matches, amateur of course. . . . Then there are moving pictures nearly every night free. So you see the boys are treated pretty well.

AUGUST 15, 1917

. . . They are enlisting coons again, now.[55] Perhaps you don't know, but they don't mix races. These are the first coons I have seen here. Perhaps they want a new division.

AUGUST 21, 1917

I have been neglecting you lately, haven't I? Another confession. Have been out on pass and didn't come up to see you. Sunday the whole squad had 24 hour passes starting at noon. I wasn't going but another fellow was just going over . . . to Coney Island. It takes about two hours to go there but it is only a 20c ride. Will tell you about the details when I come up. Now it's enough to say we didn't get back . . . till 5 a.m. We didn't have any sleep at all untill yesterday afternoon so you can imagine our condition on arrival here. Guess you'll think I'm getting to be a bum, but I have to have some excitement. That pass won't interfere with my getting another so you'll forgive me won't you Mart?

. . . This afternoon I was detailed to teach my "Wop" friend his general orders.[56] I spent about two hours on him yesterday and the same amount this afternoon. Don't you think he ought to improve rapidly. I'm sure he'll learn how to swear. Perhaps they'll enlist school teachers for the army soon. If they do you may be able to take your trip to France.

SEPTEMBER 5, 1917

. . . Pay-day to-day and I can hear dice rolling from all quarters. Also the sound of moneys changing hands. It really is funny to see what fools some people can make of themselves. Perhaps for saying that I'll become a confirmed gambler myself some day. I really am tempted to try my luck sometimes but I despise craps. Seems to me niggers must have invented it.

SEPTEMBER 23, 1917 (Camp Mills)

Reached camp safe this morning at about 1:30 but we were halted twice and asked to show our passes. I sure had a good time in the big city[,] that is after we found out where all the excitement was. After supper and mailing your letter we started walking along Broadway but actually the place was deserted. Jake didn't know any more about the city than myself so we couldn't understand it. . . . [57]

We got sick of wandering around shortly and decided to ride on the L[58] untill we found some place that looked promising. All this time we had been on lower Broadway near the water front. That's where all the big buildings are but there's nothing doing there in the evening. I asked a guy finally where the excitement was in N.Y. and he told us 42nd St. & Broadway so there we went.

It is some place up there. We went to a show "The Man Without a Country" and on account of being Sammies got seats for half price. It was terrible going back tho. The train was on time starting but we lost an hour in the scheduled forty minute run to Homestead. Stood up all the way in. The train was jammed full of soldiers.

OCTOBER 6, 1917

. . . I just now had a visit from my friend Jake. He's just been transferred to E. Co. this afternoon. You asked his nationality once I believe and I never told you. He's a Russian and a dandy guy. Been in this country only six years and has been to school quite a little. Has no relatives in this country at all. Is this too much? . . .

Good-bye my own sweetheart,
Brownie

Brownie held his relationship with Marty dear to his heart throughout his adventures. Their time apart obviously caused some problems, but it also seems to have brought them closer together as they learned to trust each other more fully and to communicate their feelings in letters. He also revealed in his letters why he felt he had to destroy those that Marty sent. His expressions of love were even more poignant.

JULY 12, 1917 (Fort Slocum)

My Own Marty,

. . . It is surprising how many things you find lacking when you go back to the primitive state. I will deserve the title "Adam", and I certainly miss my Eve.

JULY 15, 1917

. . . Your letter came last night and it did me a bunch of good to read it. Of course not as good as seeing you but next to it. All of the fellows with me have girls and we are a lonesome bunch at times. Yesterday we were considering whether we should desert or not just to see our sweet-hearts. I am not sure if that last should be one word or two, but I *am* sure that it means one girl to me. Can you guess who she is? I would tell you how much I think of her only there is not enough paper on this island. One thing that makes me lonesome more than any other is to see the girls over here see their fellows. I would rather never see one until I see you again. I don't mean that it isn't pleasant to think of you—anyway you know what I mean. "Unino"[59] that we both want to be together so that is enough. Just think of Bantam when we were together all of the time. I wish someone would get the Kaiser and then we will be to-gether won't we Marty? Do you remember our last night? Of course you do. I can't express just how I feel when I remember it. It seems so different from what I expected. To think that you are all my own. Isn't that enough? I can't write much when I write like that Marty because I have day-dreams.[60]

. . . Am going to quit now Marty, but will write again soon. I will be thinking of you to-morrow noon when you get this letter and believe me Marty "I will be loving you all of the time."

JULY 23, 1917

My pass expired at 4 this afternoon, and I was on time.[61] I wasn't going to write you tonight, but got to thinking—you know how it is—so I had to do it. I think I love you just a little to-night, Marty, and I would like to show you how much that little is. It is a LOT. . . .

I just wanted to let you know to-night that I love you just a little more that ever before.

AUGUST 12, 1917

. . . Yes, my little Eve, there are many places where you and I have been together. Have just been smiling over some of the things that happened out at Bantam.

AUGUST 22, 1917

. . . It seems someway as if I loved you more all the time. Don't feel so lonesome tho as I used to. Perhaps I'll get used to being away sometime, but I'll never stop loving you, Marty. Sometimes I dream of you and then to wake up and find it is a dream. That is the worst. I'd rather not dream.

AUGUST 31, 1917

Are you afflicted with a disease known as tonsillitis yet? If you are you may blame me. I will tell you why I write thusly. I have had it so think that perhaps you were exposed. Guess it has afflicted my memory but you may know if you were near enough to get it or not. I had a little sore throat when I was in East M. [Morris] but tho't nothing of it.[62] Last night after eating it was worse so I decided to go to the hospital to get something for it. The doctor threw his search-light down my wind pipe (I don't mean that literally) and said I'd have to go to the hospital for treatment.

SEPTEMBER 25, 1917 (Camp Mills)

Just read your Sunday letter and I know that you missed me. I'd give a good deal for a short walk with you. . . . It doesn't seem to be so fated tho. If I had enough nerve I'd come right up and let them go to the devil. . . .

The moon is getting nice again. Do you know my thoughts? When I do come up we will try to make up for it Mart. Here's a little goodnight with loads of love for one girl.

OCTOBER 6, 1917

. . . You'll have to excuse any questions I don't answer Marty and there's probably been lots lately. I havn't a place to keep them so sometimes I destroy them before answering. I love them but what else could I do? . . .

Wonder if it's dangerous to write this way. Must stop now, Marty, but am sending you lots of love and think of you.

OCTOBER 16, 1917

I'm very glad I saw you Sunday.[63] Guess my memory needed freshening. My letter yesterday was crazy but then—I was kind of inclined that way. It's hard to say good-bye but it's worth while saying it. . . .

Marty I must stop now and write home. You know how much I love you and always will wherever I am don't you Marty? . . .

Goodnight Marty,
Brownie

Brownie's letter of October 16 was the last one he wrote before embarking for France two days later, marking the end of his initial military training. When the 42nd Division set sail from the United States in mid-October, no one in the division, from Brownie to its highest-ranking officer, knew what to expect. They all recognized the challenge and probably shared a similar belief to Brownie's that "we can't shoot Germans from this island, can we?"[64] However, little did they understand how ill prepared they were for the ferocity of the fighting on the western front. While several months still remained before they would enter the trenches and experience even limited combat, they left confident they would prevail. Prevail they would, but they could have never imagined the costs.

TWO

From the States to a Quiet Sector in France

B rownie and most of the 42nd Division arrived at Saint-Nazaire, France, by November 1, 1917. One transport carrying part of the division had to return to New York after experiencing engine trouble, and those troops eventually rejoined the division in December. Brownie's experiences during his first few months in France were fairly typical of other soldiers in the AEF. He moved around a lot, faced shortages of equipment and shelter, detested the environmental conditions, trained some, and never saw the front. The division spent most of the time between November 1917 and February 1918 acclimating to France and preparing for more intensive training.

Brownie's letters from this period were noticeably less frequent. They follow the 42nd through its initial transition to France and its assignment to a quiet sector of the front, where the division trained with various French units in February 1918. While his correspondence clearly indicates how busy he was at times, his descriptions highlight deficiencies in the AEF's training program and also provide glimpses into some of the problems the soldiers faced. From the discomforts of the Atlantic crossing, to the cold and wet weather, to the travails of finding billeting,

Brownie and the rest of the Rainbow Division received a rude introduction to conditions in war-torn France.

NOVEMBER 2, 1917 (France)

My dearest Marty,

It's a long time since I sent you a letter now—so long that I hardly know how to start. To begin with I'm in France and it seems like a million miles to the U.S. and you. The trip over was not enjoyable at all tho I escaped being seasick. Can't even be sure the trip is over yet as we are still aboard the transport. Imagine it being over two weeks since I have stepped on shore. We arrived here in port at about four o'clock yesterday morning and here we are still for no one knows how long. Left Camp Mills the Thursday following our picnic and sailed from Hoboken the following morning. The first day out was beautiful but soon the boys began to be sick. Then we were allowed very little deck liberty and the heat from the Gulf Stream made the hole where we sleep terrible. We were three days passing thru that warm water. Of course the ship is crowded anyway. Then came the submarine dangers either real or unreal but very real from the precautions taken. We had drills every day and for several days could not even take off our coats or shoes to sleep. We had also to be always in reach of our life preservers. The trip across is ended at least and now remains to get off the ship. It's very trying to get here and still be confined. The buildings in sight from here appear very quaint and its useless to say that I'd love to explore the city. We are forbidden to write names and numbers and several other things. As I'm not sure about the rules they may cut out some of this letter. I wrote three letters to you but as I don't think they'd go I won't send them. . . . It's impossible to keep oneself clean here with only salt water to wash in.

NOVEMBER 19, 1917

. . . We stayed on that boat in port for about four days and had two walks ashore but no liberty. Then they took us off and shipped us in box-cars for two days and three nights. The boat was heaven compared to the train. We ate hard-tacks and canned meat and never washed or shaved or slept. I tried to sleep the third night till someone stepped on my head—then I gave it up. The landscape and houses and villages were very picturesque and we enjoyed it some in spite of conditions. The houses are all of concrete or stone and nearly always have red tile roofs. There were lots of leaves on the trees and a good many flowers were in blossom. So you see it's warmer here than in Conn. But it rains nearly every day. Really the weather is miserable nearly all the time now. Finally, we left the confounded train and hiked about five miles thru the mud to be billeted in a very small village. We recuperated there for five or six days got some of the sick men cured up then were ordered over here about fifteen miles from the first town. The Lord deliver me from many marches like that last one. Our feet always give out first. . . .

From Brownie

Brownie's description of the voyage across the Atlantic Ocean as "not enjoyable at all" is the ultimate understatement. Moving an army from the United States to Europe was extremely difficult. How to transport the AEF to Europe was one of the fundamental questions the United States faced when it declared war.[1] The assistant secretary of war recalled, "The War Department set forth upon its great troop-ferrying enterprise without any ships at all; at least without any suitable ones."[2] Since the United States did not own sufficient numbers of ships to transport the AEF, it had to find and/or build as many ships as possible and depend on its allies for help. The German U-boat campaign compounded the problem: roughly twenty-five percent of the ships that sailed from the United States for Europe in the first half of 1917 failed to return safely.[3] However, none of the troop transports carrying men to France was lost.

Over the course of 1917, the United States mobilized its merchant fleet, began construction on new vessels, and seized German ships docked in American harbors at the time of the declaration of war. Out of more than ninety German ships that were confiscated, twenty were used to transport almost 560,000 soldiers to Europe. The United States eventually managed to ship more than 2 million soldiers to Europe in eighty-six separate convoys. British ships carried 49 percent of them; U.S. vessels, including the confiscated German vessels, transported 43 percent; and other countries moved the rest.[4]

Considering the total number of troops who sailed to Europe,

Brownie was one of the first to arrive. A total of 116,261 soldiers left the United States for Europe by the end of October 1917. Brownie also sailed from the main port of embarkation in the United States, Hoboken, New Jersey, in New York harbor. His division represented about half the troops who went to Europe by sailing directly to France. Most of the rest temporarily stopped in England.[5]

The 42nd Division sailed on October 18 aboard three big liners and four smaller transports. Brownie's 117th Engineers Regiment sailed on the USS *Covington*, formerly the German liner *Cincinnati* of the Hamburg-American line. The trip typically took about two weeks and the Rainbow division's experience was no exception. The five thousand men on the *Covington* shared the same schedule and experiences as their comrades on other ships. Reveille was at 6:00 a.m., breakfast at 6:30, inspection at 10:30, lunch at noon, inspection just before sunset, dinner at 5:00, and lights out at 9:00. While the schedule seems pretty light, it was anything but that; the soldiers often had to stand in line for hours to get food, experienced repeated "abandon ship" drills, and were only allowed on deck generally for one hour or less a day.[6]

The rules on the ship were pretty straightforward. You were supposed to wait patiently, sleep in your assigned berth, keep your life preserver with you at all times, be alert for submarines, avoid accidents, and make sure your weapons remained unloaded.[7] Unfortunately for the men, the ships were dreadfully overcrowded. One soldier exclaimed, "Soldiers everywhere, no place to sit, no place to stand. A nice brisk walk? Impossible. . . . Oh for the roominess of a sardine can."[8] Another doughboy remembered that the men were "crowded like horses into narrow bunks, with the plainest of food, in total darkness at night, denied even the solace of a cigarette except by daylight, always having boat drills—it was the Rainbow Division's first test in stern discipline."[9] The limited food preparation facilities and the fact that many men had never sailed on the ocean before compounded the overcrowded conditions.

These complications can be seen most clearly in the recommendation from the 42nd Division's commander concerning future trips: "Suitable vomit cans or buckets should be placed in sufficient numbers" to meet the needs of the men.[10] Col. George Leach, the commander of the division's 151st Field Artillery Regiment, captured the reasons for this recommendation in his diary entries describing the conditions on his ship:

> Friday, October 19–6,000 men on-board; men allowed on deck 45 min. twice a day; The air below deck is getting very bad and men are sick; the holds are tough places to live.
> Saturday, October 20—Sea is rough and most men are sick. . . . The hold and decks at times look simply hopeless with filth. . . .
> Friday, October 26—It is cold and cloudy and hard to keep warm, the wind being very raw.
> Saturday, October 27—From now on we will be in acute submarine and mine danger zone.[11]

On another ship, a soldier reported, "the floors were covered with the vomit of troops who had yet to find their sea legs."[12]

The low quality of the food and the difficulty at times of getting three meals a day made the seasickness worse. Soldiers complained that it was so crowded that they sometimes only got one meal a day.[13] The commander of the ambulance section of the 117th Sanitary Train described the conditions onboard ship as "nothing short of vile." He added that it was "impossible for the men to even keep an outward appearance of cleanliness. Beans last night were sour and this morning there was a resulting diarrhea. The seating capacity of the water closets under normal conditions are so inadequate that men stand for hours waiting to relieve themselves."[14]

It is impossible to determine which ship carrying the 42nd Division had the worst conditions, but the *Mallory*, one of the smaller transports, had to have been one of them. Ned Harden, another Rainbow Division soldier, explained, "Hollow pipe bunks with canvas strips laced across them made up the bed. . . . Over 1300 men had to be fed three meals a day, a formidable task. Bilge water, steam, rancid butter, potato peelings, beans, frozen beef and beef a little spoiled, baking bread and fresh dough, rotten cigars and seasick men was the setting for eating meals. . . . to the landlubbers it was pure HELL, in capital letters."[15]

Another *Mallory* veteran recalled, "Who will ever forget the peculiar sensation of sliding across the mess hall, scattering slum in all directions, and ending up with a dismal splash in two feet of bilge water. Our food, too—what a wonderfully fragrant mess."[16]

Maybe the War Department could be excused for subjecting soldiers to these difficulties when everything was still in transition early in the war, but conditions on the transports unfortunately did not change over the next year. Pvt. W. G. Hudson, a replacement soldier for the First Division who crossed the Atlantic in April 1918, believed on his ship that "pigs were better off."[17] Another doughboy recorded in his diary his experience crossing the English Channel in June 1918: "We are packed on this boat like hogs going to market; the sea is rough we are tossed & tossed the whole night; Get so sick a few hours out. Ye Gods! I am sick! I try & get out on deck; just have to wade and climb over the ones on the floor. The latrines are full of sea sick ones too; Can't step without stepping in throw-up."[18]

The sight of land offered relief to every soldier on the transports, but most of them ended up spending additional nights onboard ship before they were able to disembark. This problem resulted from several factors, including inadequate docking facilities and the desire to off-load equipment first. As Brownie's letters indicate, the 42nd Division ran into this difficulty when it arrived at Saint-Nazaire. Unfortunately, the French port's facilities were not prepared for the influx of American soldiers, and many troops had to remain onboard their transports for days after their arrival.[19]

While limited port facilities proved to be the main reason soldiers could not disembark as quickly as they hoped, there were also other factors. Brownie did not describe some of the entertainment the soldiers sought ashore, but it proved a major problem. One reason why the soldiers remained onboard ship so long was for officers to arrange transportation to get troops away from Saint-Nazaire as quickly as possible. The American commander and his staff knew that the city was a hot spot for prostitution, that men arriving in Europe had not seen women for a long time, and that one of the leading causes for the debilitation of soldiers in the British and French armies was the proliferation of venereal diseases.[20] General Pershing had reason to worry because many of the men in the 42nd were very interested in the local women. Seventy years after the war, one former private was asked, "What forms of off-duty recreation were common?" He answered, "Wine, women, & song." To the follow-up question, "Was there much consorting with local women?" he responded, "Whenever possible."[21]

The legendary escapades of many men in the Rainbow Division while on pass in Saint-Nazaire possibly led Pershing to take the threat of the spread of venereal diseases even more seriously than he already did.[22] The venereal disease rate in the regular army was 90 cases per 1,000 soldiers prior to U.S. involvement in World War I. The First and Second Divisions, the initial AEF troops in Europe, had a rate of 40 per 1,000. In early November the rate in the AEF skyrocketed to 200 per 1,000.[23]

The men of the 42nd did not go ashore without some awareness of what they might meet. In fact, many went quite readily. Before the doughboys were able to leave the ships, the Rainbow officers challenged the men to maintain "high standards of conduct," and while enjoying "the freedom of the town, they should refrain from excesses that might injure the reputation of the command."[24] As the old saying goes, the warnings "went in one ear and out the other." Leslie Langville, a member of one of the 42nd Division's field artillery regiments, remembered, "Before anyone got off, we were subjected to a lecture by First Lieutenant George Gould in the art of protecting our manly virtues. According to the lieutenant, we were in much danger of being raped the minute we put one foot on French soil. Most of the fellows would have been very willing victims of such treatment."[25]

While there is no indication that Brownie ever indulged in these activities, it is clear that many of his comrades did. Alcohol was plentiful and there were seemingly prostitutes around every corner.[26] Frank Kolar wrote in his diary on November 4, "The comfort stations are rather public but nevertheless answer the purpose. Wild night up to 11 o'clock. All were either drunk or in jail."[27] Dr. Hugh Young, one of the AEF's leading medical officers, provided a vivid description in his autobiography of the prevalence of prostitution in Saint-Nazaire: "The situation within [the whorehouses] was terrible. The line of soldiers waiting their turn extended along the narrow hall to the individual doorways. . . . One [Madame] proudly told me that her most active girl had taken care of sixty-five the day before, and that the average was between forty and fifty per day." Young asked dumbfounded, "But how can they stand such a terrific experience? Oh, monsieur, they wear out in about four weeks. We ship them off to less popular joints and before long they are completely used up and become streetwalkers." Young concluded that as bad as this situation was, it became even worse because of "the fact that by receiving one individual after another without any douching or even rising from their beds, these women came to possess 'septic tanks' filled with almost every type of venereal infection."[28]

Whether the result of the Rainbow Division's activities or not, the AEF witnessed a whirlwind of discussion and resulting changes in regulations to combat venereal diseases within a few weeks of the division's passage through Saint-Nazaire. Unlike America's allies, Pershing decided against trying to regulate prostitution and instead made it off-limits wherever possible.[29] One of the first steps was to offer suitable alternative forms of entertainment. "Constant efforts will be made to provide amusements, interest and occupations for the soldiers and civilian employees when off duty. Reading rooms, entertainments, opportunity for athletic sports, etc. will be offered whenever and wherever practicable."[30] The second was to increase the consequences of contracting a venereal disease by increasing punishments for those who became infected. A special order in November 1917 threatened that any soldier contracting venereal diseases would have to forfeit his pay while incapacitated. Furthermore, an infected soldier faced the prospects of a court-martial. Third, Pershing made officers more responsible for their men's well-being by questioning whether units with high venereal disease rates had effective leaders. Finally, military police were stationed at known houses of prostitution to prevent American soldiers from indulging.[31]

Cracking down on venereal diseases also required closer inspections of the soldiers themselves; therefore, Pershing ordered all soldiers to be inspected bimonthly, if at all possible, by a medical officer.[32] For the men this meant the unforgettable "short-arm inspection." One soldier exclaimed, "The indignity of indignities was the 'short arm inspection.' These inspections were unannounced and all personnel undergoing the inspection were required to strip from the waist down and stand on his footlocker . . . to be inspected by the medical officer."[33]

Soldiers who engaged in risky behaviors were also ordered to report to the nearest prophylaxis station for treatment within hours of exposure. In the treatment, "the external genital organs were first to be thoroughly washed with a solution of bichloride of mercury and then 4 cc. of argyrol was injected into the urethra with 'an ordinary penis syringe,' the solution to remain 'for full five minutes'; finally, the entire penis was smeared with two grams of calomel ointment and 'allowed to remain undisturbed.'"[34] Altogether, the medical teams of the AEF administered 242,000 prophylaxis treatments during the war. Even with these efforts, more than seventy-three thousand soldiers in the AEF were placed on the sick report because of venereal diseases.[35]

Pershing's and the AEF's policies ran into opposition from the French. Many French women relied on prostitution for their livelihood. French premier Georges Clemenceau even wrote a letter to Pershing offering to build "clean" houses of prostitution where the women would be inspected regularly.[36] Other than being morally appalled, Pershing knew the French inspections were superficial at best. Pershing's own medical officers found that French inspectors had examined fifty-nine women in one hour in Bordeaux, fifteen in thirteen minutes in Cherbourg, and forty in fifty minutes in Paris. Additionally, "at Bordeaux the same speculum was used on each woman, without being cleaned; in other words, it was taken out of the vagina of one woman and immediately introduced into that of another."[37]

Surprisingly, the AEF's efforts were remarkably successful. By early January 1918, the venereal disease rate had fallen to 16 cases per 1,000 and by September it was down to 1 case per 1,000.[38] This does not mean, however, that soldiers could not find women when given the opportunity. One member of the 42nd recalled that in February 1918 "we encountered our first ladies of the night since landing in France, and some of us had an introduction to sex with a capital 'S'."[39] While the AEF may have won the battle against venereal disease, it did not necessarily change its soldiers' desires.

Attempting to control American soldiers' sexual appetites remained an ever-present problem, but the AEF's main focus was preparing its men to face combat in the trenches. One of the most significant initial problems in doing this was actually transporting the soldiers from their ports of arrival to specified training areas, generally in northeastern France. Ultimately, most of the soldiers traveled on the infamous French railroad cars, better known as Hommes 40, Chevaux 8. As Brownie noted in one of his letters, "The boat was heaven compared to the train." These boxcars supposedly could carry either forty men or eight horses, but as one soldier recalled, they were "crowded and uncomfortable as hell." [40] Besides being crowded, the cars posed several other unique problems including sleeping and the lack of sanitary facilities. One soldier remembered, "Sleep was practically impossible with the cramped conditions and penetrating cold." [41] Another described the boxcars as "so crowded we had to sleep spoon fashion—when one turned over, all had to turn." [42]

Relieving themselves posed an even more vexing problem than sleeping. General orders called for placing one garbage can or two buckets and a box of sand in each car. [43] With the crowded conditions, these facilities proved inadequate on most trips; therefore, the soldiers often found other ways to take care of bodily functions. A sergeant in the Thirty-fifth Division later wrote,

> There were of course no toilet facilities and only two announced rest stops, one about midnight and one at noon the following day. Urination was no problem, just a case of involuntary indecent exposure in full view of the admiring populace. . . .
>
> The constipated were fortunate. The poor devil who just had to go linked hands with a pair of carefully chosen muscular friends who braced themselves while he swung his tail out into the breeze and shuddered at the sight of the ties and gravel whizzing by below his bared butt. [44]

While the soldiers had to worry about the lack of physical comforts during transit, Pershing and his staff busily pursued organizing the AEF. Unbeknownst to Brownie or other AEF soldiers, the Rainbow Division's future as a cohesive unit was in doubt because Pershing found the National Guard contemptible. He had observed the inadequate training of most National Guard units during the 1916 Mexican excursion and also believed their organization in local communities encouraged corruption and favoritism. [45] Since the 42nd was a National Guard unit and also included recent enlistees and draftees, the AEF's commander thought it should be disbanded and the troops used to fill out other divisions. Pershing and his staff contemplated dissolving the division in November 1917. Fortunately, the division's unique origins and popularity at home precluded its dismemberment. One possible result of Pershing's disfavor, however, was the replacement of the division's commanding officer, Gen. William Mann, with Maj. Gen. Charles T. Menoher, a career officer who had graduated from West Point and who was well liked by Pershing.[46]

NOVEMBER 25, 1917 (France)

Dearest Marty,

. . . I wish you could see these little towns over here. If we had towns like this and all the others I've seen around here we'd expect everyone to die. By that I mean the sanitary conditions are bad. This is a farming country but unlike the U.S. the farmers all live in a little town. The buildings are never separate either— they all are built together like in a city. Even the barns are right in the houses. For a fact you cannot tell the barn door from the front door in lots of cases. Then the refuse pile from the barn and house both is usually in the front yard. . . .

The boys are doing some work on building barracks but it doesn't amount to much. I've had it lucky here. You know I've studied French some so can get along pretty well talking this lingo. I'm in town nearly all the time, buying things, hiring teams, etc. There doesn't seem to be anyone else in the company who can speak a word so you may see I am pretty busy sometimes. If this keeps up I'll be a regular Frenchman soon.

DECEMBER 20, 1917

. . . I don't know how often I'll be able to write because sometimes we have no place to write in. Now I'm writing in a private house. That is one of the benefits I receive, parce que je peut parler Francaise. In fact about all I do now is to talk French. I've been going around lately with my old friend Rondilone.[47] He and I are the only ones in the company who can talk French at all and we can get anything we want.

. . . We are very numerous over here now and in fact consider it wonderful how well we are fed and clothed and supplied. And at that a soldier in my position can't begin to understand the difficulties of transportation and all. . . . . Anyway, I just want to tell you that the longer I'm here the more spirit I have to "stick it out" for the good of humanity and the U.S. which is the same thing. . . . It's really not as bad as that tho it's hard to find time sometimes. You've no idea . . . how much attention our feet require. Not that I need them to write with but attention requires time. Ask Alida if that book ever said anything about marching twenty kilometers in hobnailed shoes and the results.[48] Frost-bites, blisters, and wet feet for a week might make up three chapters in the volume I'm going to write. But you don't have to worry about that cause if they get bad enough so you can't walk at all—why you can stay in quarters for two or three days—usually damp and without a fire.

FEBRUARY 8, 1918

. . . Yes, I'm now quite experienced as regards "cooties" I'm sorry to tell you.[49] In fact, they're quite common thruout the entire company. . . . Have to stick it out tho, Marty for more reasons than one. . . .

Your own,

Brownie

As the AEF's high command debated the 42nd Division's future, the doughboys began a series of seemingly constant moves. Between November 1917 and the middle of February 1918, Brownie's engineering regiment visited several different training areas, including the towns of Vaucouleurs and Rolampont and numerous villages.[50] Pershing even admitted in January 1918 that the 42nd's movements had hampered its training.[51] While the division occasionally moved by train, it generally marched to any new destination. In this regard, Brownie and the other engineers sometimes had advantages over the average doughboy. Since the engineers often moved ahead of the other forces to prepare the new location for the division's arrival, they sometime were able to ride trains while others had to walk.[52] Also, Brownie's seemingly unique ability within his company to speak French resulted in him being assigned special tasks. As one historian notes, "Any Yank who knew a little French was in great demand."[53]

These special circumstances allowed Brownie to miss one of the most notorious events in the division's history. On December 26 the division began a four-day march of more than sixty miles. The distance should not have been a problem since the soldiers were used to marching nearly fifteen miles a day, but the weather, lack of experience, and inadequate equipment and supplies caused difficulties. One officer recalled that the march "appears one of the most trying and arduous with which the division was ever confronted." He added, "In a blinding snow storm it commenced. The roads were deep with snow, with a treacherous glassy base and full of long grades and sharp turns. The thermometer kept on dropping and the men proceeded through these conditions in the same uniform in which they passed review before the Secretary of War [in September at Camp Mills]."[54] Another doughboy added that the men's "shoes wore out—men were marching barefooted through the snow sometimes; they wrapped bags around their feet and kept on. There were bloody footprints along the route of the column. At night they pulled up in some little village and slept—exhausted heaps of frozen men huddling together in barns and haylofts."[55] If the weather and poor quality of the soldiers' boots were not bad enough, some of the doughboys had to subsist on two light meals a day.[56]

After this grueling march, the soldiers moved into their training areas where they had to come to grips with the poor living conditions. Although their views modified over time as the soldiers realized how much suffering the French had experienced, at first they "shared a near-universal conviction that the French were a filthy people who lived amid manure piles and relieved themselves in public."[57] One soldier described his first impressions of France, "What a depressing sight it was! A handful of houses, some in a ruined condition from previous air raids, huge piles of manure in front of every dwelling, and the streets in an unkempt condition."[58] The soldiers had to deal with these conditions directly since as Brownie reveals, they had to find billets in the villages at least until barracks could be constructed.[59] One doughboy wrote home that "there are three classes of inhabitants in these homes—first, residents; second, cattle; third, soldiers."[60]

Soldiers often billeted in barns with the animals, creating, as one Rainbow veteran remembered, some unique problems. "Having to descend a straight ladder in a barn and pass the rear-ends of eight or ten ill-mannered, ill-tempered horses was no easy feat."[61]

These conditions were magnified by other problems, in particular a marked shortage of supplies and clothing.[62] Col. Johnson Hagood, commander of the advanced section of the supply service, recalled that in the fall of 1917 "the supplies of the 42nd Division, at Vaucouleurs, were scattered out over a ten-acre field, most of it in the open and in such condition that it could not be segregated nor used. This division had only six trucks to distribute troops and supplies over a billeting area of about eighteen square miles."[63] Since there were more than twenty thousand men in the division at this point, each vehicle had the impossible task of supplying more than three thousand soldiers. The conditions only grew worse, as late fall and winter of 1917 were cold and wet. One soldier in Brownie's company said "it was awfully cold for a while and we didn't see the ground for over five weeks for the snow. It was three or four feet deep at times."[64] If the soldiers had had the proper uniform, the weather would not have been as serious a concern.

In addition to the cold and wet weather, the soldiers had to deal with the basic inconvenience of limited sanitary facilities. At more permanent stops "the latrine was simply a deep trench, with a wooden cover, which had more or less wide slots to be opened for use. It had a canvas fence around it."[65] On the move the soldiers simply used the surrounding countryside.

Soldiers faced significant health risks because of these adverse conditions. The environment created a breeding ground for numerous disease-carrying parasites such as fleas and lice, a particular nuisance for any soldier serving in the trenches.[66] A member of the Rainbow's trench mortar battery recalled that "year round there were 'cooty' or bodylice. Lice were ubiquitous throughout all troops at all ranks, and so a portable boiler was taken around to the front once a month to sterilize the men's clothes. The soldiers had to wait naked and shivering until their uniforms, now stiff and wrinkled, were returned. By next morning they were invariably lousy again."[67] The following poem, written by a soldier, captures the essence of the lice problem:

With a manner quite invidious,
And an attitude insidious,
He will plant himself upon a mortal's frame,
And with gimlet, pike, and augur,
And the cant-hook of a logger,
He will do his best to viscerate and maim.

Since the days of ancient Rome,
The human body's been his home,
A sort of perennial sacred niche;
And he chuckles with great pleasure
As you dance the cootie measure
To the gleeful time of his eternal itch.

He dotes on Yank and French,
And the English in the trench
He cares not for a permanent location;
But when he finds a human,
All his friends and he start roamin',
And establish a splendid habitation.

And when it seems that coals of fire
And that flaming darts aspire
To seek an inlet to your very heart,
Stop your scratching just to reason
That this is cootie season,
And your body's now a busy cootie mart.[68]

Besides causing incessant itching, the lice carried diseases like typhus and trench fever that could gravely weaken the men in the ranks.[69]

Diseases and other illnesses, whether carried by lice or something else, plagued the AEF. The following illnesses and diseases reached at times epidemic proportions: measles, mumps, scarlet fever, cerebrospinal meningitis, small pox, typhoid, paratyphoid A and B, diphtheria, tetanus, influenza, venereal diseases, and typhus fever.[70] Shortages of supplies and medical personnel compounded these problems, and medical personnel "found that it was entirely inadequate to care for the men. . . . The Medical detachment was at a loss to know how to care for the large amount of sickness in the Battalion caused by the inclement weather, poor sanitary conditions, poor billets and lack of facilities for drying clothing."[71]

JANUARY 6, 1918 (France)

My dearest Marty,

. . . I'll have to tell you the news of my new job and it's some job, too. I was made a Corporal night before last and as a result I have seven men to look after. It's much easier to be a "Buck Private" but one can't turn down advancement. So now I wear two stripes and attend non-com meetings daily. The meetings are interesting but we are pretty tired usually. We are drilling hard & working hard now, but as it's all for the U.S. it's O.K.

JANUARY 28, 1918

. . . After supper it's non-com school and to-night there were personal history cards to make out. Not only my own but I have to see to it that my squad make them out too. And now I'm waiting each moment for taps to blow when lights have to go out. See the mental strain I'm under don't you? Really it's worrisome to find time for everything but that's one thing I like about the army. Nearly everything takes care of itself here. . . . Now I'm insured for $10,000. Worth more dead than alive. . . . Not that I expect to die but it's also valuable in case one is injured and disabled.

FEBRUARY 14, 1918

. . . This is quite a town and as our advance guard hit it on Mardi Gras we were lucky. The French people were having their festival masquerading and all. It must be pretty nice in time of peace. Our company has been here before so I visited all my friends and naturally helped them eat up some of their good things. My memory fails me about some of the things that happened but it was the best time I've had in France so far. Yesterday the company came in so we had to come back to earth again. To make it more of a reality we all drew helmets in the afternoon and as they took away our hats we have to wear the former. Don't know as you ever saw a helmet cause I never did till I got to France. They're bad things to wear as they weigh about two and a half pounds. You can bump your head pretty hard with one on tho & and not feel it much. It looks funny to see all the troops with helmets on. It's hard to recognize one's friends now, and if he puts on his mask you never can tell him.

Must tell you about our experience with gas. Our regiment had a small chamber constructed to go around to the different companies on a truck. Just to test out our masks also to let us know how it smells. First we went thru with our English masks on. They are the best as the air comes to your lungs perfectly pure no matter how thick the gas. This mask has a little tin box attached to it that the air has to pass thru. There are chemicals in the box which purify the air. The second time we went thru the chamber with our French masks. [72] That also is a good mask but the chemicals are on the face piece itself. The air has to pass thru the cloth and padding and imagine the smell. It's also more stuffy than the English mask. However, it's very simple. The gas we had in the chamber was simply tear gas so they let us go into it without any masks at all. It had a very peculiar smell but affects the eyes mostly. . . .

From your own,

Brownie

Pershing laid the framework for how the AEF was to be trained while soldiers dealt with the problems caused by insufficient supplies, the weather, and the overall environment. Pershing operated based on the guidance he received in his initial instructions from President Wilson: "In military operations against the imperial German government you are directed to cooperate with the forces of the other countries employed against the enemy; but in so doing the underlying idea must be kept in view that the forces of the United States are a separate and distinct component of the combined forces, the identity of which must be preserved." [73]

From Pershing's perspective, his instructions meant the American forces would not be integrated or amalgamated with British or French units besides in training, "except in case of absolute necessity." [74] He laid out three principle objections to amalgamation: "first, troops would lose their national identity; second, they probably could not be relieved for service with us without disrupting the Allied divisions to which assigned, especially if engaged in active service; third, the methods of training and instruction in both Allied armies are very different from our own which would produce some confusion at the start and also when troops returned to service with us."[75] The instructions did not mean, however, that Pershing would not cooperate with the allies.[76]

Pershing's third objection played a central role in the AEF's training. He had in mind that the American way of war would be quite different from what he saw as the stale tactics of the British and the French. He described his proposed tactics as "open warfare." Unfortunately, he never clearly translated what that meant for the actual training of the AEF.[77] The closest he came was issuing combat instructions in September 1918:

> French warfare is marked by uniform formations, the reg-
> ulation of space and time by higher command down to the
> smallest details, absence of scouts preceding the first wave,
> fixed distances and intervals between units and individuals,
> voluminous orders, careful rehearsal, little initiative upon
> the part of the individual soldier. Open warfare is marked
> by scouts who precede the first wave, irregularity of forma-
> tion, comparatively little regulation of space and time by
> higher command, the greatest possible use of the infantry's
> own fire power to enable it to get forward, variable distance
> and intervals between units and individuals, use of every
> form of cover and accident of ground during the advance,
> brief orders, and the greatest possible use of individual
> initiative by all troops engaged in the action.[78]

What Pershing never fully understood, or at least showed an ap-
preciation for, was that to achieve the prerequisites for open warfare, an army had to first break the stalemate of the trenches.[79]

Although there was some confusion as to how the AEF should
be trained, and the soldiers faced many difficulties just acclimating to the western front, each division did begin a training program once in France. This training was critical since in November 1917 Pershing considered the AEF ill prepared for service in
the trenches. He did say he would rush troops to the trenches if
the Allies were about to collapse but this would be "a desperate
measure."[80]

In training the AEF, Pershing insisted that standards be the same as those at West Point.[81] Beyond discipline, the training was supposed to emphasize "the assumption of a vigorous offensive" and that "the rifle and the bayonet are the principle weapons of the infantry soldier."[82] The AEF's initial training program involved three separate phases: training in camps with each division broken into component parts, instruction in trenches in a quiet sector, and finally, division training with an emphasis on large-scale maneuvers. After this training, a division was supposed to take over a sector in the trenches.[83] While this program did not last beyond the German offensives beginning in March 1918, it was generally followed by the 42nd Division.

When they were not moving to a new location, the men of the 42nd trained more than forty hours a week, with the emphasis of the training gradually evolving from smaller unit activities to larger ones. Soldiers trained at the individual, squad, and platoon levels during the first three weeks. The second three weeks consisted of drills in company formations, and the third three-week period emphasized training at the battalion level. Two weeks were then spent in regimental training and another two in brigade formations. The final two weeks were devoted to coordinating the various units within a division. Most of the Rainbow, although dispersed to different villages, followed this schedule while training in northeast France near Vaucouleurs and Rolampont.[84]

The division's training and work schedules were fairly vigorous when it was not on the move. One officer reported that "the drill under the eyes of French and American instructors included artillery, machine-guns, rifles, pistols, trench-mortars and 37 millimeter-gun target practice; bayonet and gas drills, digging trenches, building shelters and wire entanglements, roads and bridges; visual and mechanical signaling and the art and science of liaison; maneuvers and terrain problems, disciplinary drill of many sorts, grenade throwing and marches."[85] The diarist of the Rainbow's 117th Field Signal Battalion recorded in December 1917, "Drill was resumed, and to drill all day in the snow, only to return to icy cold billets, at night, is anything but a pleasant experience."[86] For all of the division's activities, the AEF commander still considered the division unprepared for combat and in need of more training even in late February 1918.[87]

The activities of Brownie's engineering regiment provide a

fuller picture of some of the division's duties and responsibilities. When the United States entered the war in April 1917 there were only 3,000 engineers in the army. By November 1918 there were almost 400,000.[88] They were either assigned to the Corps of Engineers or to 1,660-man regiments within each infantry division. Brownie was in Company A, one of the six companies that made up each regiment. When he was promoted to corporal in January 1918, he became one of forty at that rank in his company.[89]

In the very early stages of U.S. involvement in the war, the engineers' principal duty was seen as building field fortifications and to a lesser extent constructing roads and buildings. However, it quickly became apparent that divisional engineers required infantry training as well.[90] The engineers ultimately had to become adept in many different skills. William Parsons, who wrote an excellent early history of the engineers in the AEF, aptly captured the variety of duties they performed:

> With each division and forming an integral part of it, was one regiment of engineers. . . . This regiment executed all construction work that was assigned to a division or to any of its component brigades. It maintained the local lines of communication, sited and dug trenches, laid out and built forward defense works, and strung the barbed wire entanglements, erected temporary small bridges, made surveys, drained camps, and did all the things of a structural nature required by the men on the fighting line. In the case of an advance, the engineers went forward with the division bridging streams, repairing roads, consolidating the captured enemy positions by reversing their face and repairing shell damage and erecting new wire entanglements.[91]

From November 1917 to mid-February 1918, when they were not moving from one location to another, the engineers spent most of their time engaged in construction projects. The engineers moved frequently until November 20, and their main job was sorting equipment. From then until December 9 they built a hospital, barracks, mess halls, and target ranges. For the rest of December the engineers regiment was attached to the Services of Supply and the men primarily constructed barracks and bath-

4. Engineers working on road in France. Courtesy of the General Douglas MacArthur Foundation.

houses.[92] In January they worked in forty different towns and villages building barracks and horse stables. They also followed "a limited drill schedule, consisting of rifle practice, practice marches and close order drill,"[93] as well as doing some "engineer training in trench warfare."[94] The regiment spent the first half of February doing similar duties.[95]

Not surprisingly, the engineers' busy construction schedules left them little time to train as infantry. To make matters worse, throughout most of these months many of the regiment's officers, including the two battalion commanders, were gone at least five weeks for specialized training courses. As with the overall division, official inspections found the regiment unfit for frontline combat duties. Lt. Col. L. H. Watkins, who inspected the regiment, discovered that two companies had never fired their guns and none of the companies had trained with hand grenades.[96]

NOVEMBER 2, 1917 (France)

My dearest Marty,

It's a long time since I sent you a letter now—so long that I hardly know how to start. To begin with I'm in France and it seems like a million miles to the U.S. and you. . . .

And what about you this time Marty? My mail is perhaps on the ocean now. I'd often be on my bunk when coming over trying to imagine just what you were doing. I figured that by the next Monday you'd be sure I'd left Camp Mills. I kept N.Y. time so I could tell somewhere near what you'd be about. Things like that help too, Marty. It's funny what little things one can remember when there is lots of time to think. There's no use saying how much I miss you and the good times we used to have. I'm just waiting to get back to Conn. My *great* natural love for the Kaiser is not increasing in the least.[97]

NOVEMBER 19, 1917

This is my second attempt to write you since we left the boat. It's no use cursing the luck of having my letters censored, I suppose. One of our lieutenants read my first letter to you and returned it because it contained too much information concerning our whereabouts. I was sore in the first place because it's bad enough to let someone you know read one anyway. I'm going to send all letters via the base censor at Paris from now on.

I'm with the A.E. Forces now Marty and you are in the U.S. No one can imagine how much I miss you every day always. Lately, I've taken to dreaming of you at night. For the last three nights in succession. It seems as if I were with you but had to leave soon to come here. One time I was trying to get someone to marry us but couldn't seem to find one. Once this war is over I'll never let you out of my sight. Guess I'll stay by the fire for six months steady. The last time I was with you seems like it was years ago already. I never answered the letter in which you asked me if I were serious about wanting to marry you that last Sunday. I really don't know myself. I wish I'd married you long ago for a fact. . . . You'll marry me when I come back anyway won't you Marty?

NOVEMBER 25, 1917

. . . The future is a funny thing isn't? I wonder where you and I will be a year from now. I never was so anxious for the war to end before. Not that I don't want to go to the front cause really

I'd like to "do my bit" seeing I'm over here. Unino why this war should end, isn't it so my Marty? I almost hate to write any more it's so uncertain when you'll get the letters. I wonder if you have ever heard from me since I left Camp Mills and without doubt you are wondering the same thing. But I've heard from you only yesterday. It was written on "Wed. Eve." October 16th. Just think how long it took. If it takes as long for this to reach you that will be next year. It did me lots of good, tho. I guess the trouble was with the address. I never had any instructions to change my address so never did it. In fact I'm not certain if I know just what it should be yet. I think its Co. A. 1 1 7 Engrs. A.E.F. c/o N.Y. P.M. [Post Master]. They don't seem to want even the name France on them. I'll write the address on every letter because the Lord only knows if you get all I write. I'm going to keep on writing tho in hopes that some day I'll get an answer to a letter I wrote from here. . . . Some day probably I'll get about fifteen letters at once.

. . . I don't know when this letter will be mailed. Now I save up my letters and send them in only large envelope to the Base Censor. Won't take any more chances with our officers. . . .

Tis now the evening of the 26th and sure enough there were two letters from you last night. And some letters, too Marty. I can't explain how I feel about both the letters and your own self. . . . Marty, I can't see how you can love me but I know you do. Does that sound funny? I've always felt that way since unino. Isn't it going to be Heaven to be together once more? You'll wait for me my own Marty, won't you? . . .

I must tell you something of what we are doing here and try to keep inside the lines—uno. Get that new word, or isn't that new for us? You see I write on only one side of the paper so the censor can cut-out what he wishes. He may get so mad at this long letter that he'll cut it all out or again you may get some of the pieces.

DECEMBER 30, 1917

I'm lying in bed to write this letter it's so confounded cold here. Just had to write to-night cause I've been reading some of your last letters this p.m. When I do read them I always feel as if I'd been neglecting you. Perhaps you know something of how it is with us here and so forgive me. Please try to forget how much I ought to write and just wait to have me tell you how much I love you.

JANUARY 28, 1918

. . . I must write you at once, convenient or not—Reasons are many—one because lately I've received so many letters from you. Also recently came the box containing the sweater, helmet, socks, and all the other numerous articles. Musn't forget the candy as that is such a treat "over here." . . .

Here's heaps of love to the best girl I ever knew or ever will know.

FEBRUARY 14, 1918

. . . Well Marty I'm going to quit now but never forget what unino. I should think the Kaiser would be ashamed of himself—keeping so many sweethearts, apart. . . .

From your own,
Brownie

What must not be lost in the discussions of the soldiers' drills, work, and living conditions are the strains the war placed on the relationships between the doughboys and their friends, families, spouses, and lovers back home. Brownie's letters reveal the difficulties of communicating in an environment where letters were censored, the destination for the mail was in flux, and there was no means of contact beyond the written word. His desire to receive letters reflected a desire held by all soldiers regardless of nationality. Most soldiers eagerly awaited mail call and experienced the gamut of emotions ranging from joy to despair depending on whether they received any mail or not.[98]

The experiences of Brownie, the 117th Engineers, and the rest of the 42nd Division during their first few months in France indicate the difficulties the AEF and the individual soldiers faced as the United States built an army from a very limited foundation. Despite its shortcomings, however, the 42nd Division was one of the better-prepared divisions in the AEF in early 1918. Although the United States had been in the war almost a year, few of its men had seen combat and most were judged insufficiently trained at best. [99] Brownie and the 42nd Division, prepared or not, were about to see their experiences in France change drastically as they were assigned to the trenches in a quiet sector for more realistic training in mid-February.

THREE

Training and Action in a Quiet Sector

The 42nd Division began active training in the trenches in the Lunéville sector of northeastern France in late February 1918. Although this area had seen fierce fighting earlier in the war, both the Germans and the French now sent units there for rest and to receive replacements before sending them back to more active sectors of the front. General Pershing and the French believed that this was the perfect area to initiate the American soldiers in the techniques of trench warfare without exposing them to too much danger of being overrun. The plan called for American units to receive training and guidance from the French forces before ultimately being placed in the trenches by themselves. The Rainbow Division engaged in training exercises with the French Eighth Army and the Seventh French Army Corps for approximately a month.[1]

The division's training program changed dramatically after the Germans began a series five offensives: Somme, March 21–April 6; Lys, April 9–27; Aisne, May 27–June 5; Montdidier-Noyon, June 9–13; and Champagne-Marne, July 15–18. The Germans launched the first offensive on March 21 with the hope of winning important victories before new American forces tipped the balance in favor of the Allies. At the beginning of the offensive the Germans had a manpower advantage over the Allies of 1,569,000 to 1,245,000.[2] However, the Germans knew that their advantage would be fleeting as more Americans arrived that summer.

The Somme offensive had a great influence on the course of the war. For the Germans it marked a last, desperate gamble to achieve victory. For the Allies it threatened potential defeat. They were so concerned about being defeated that they set aside many of their differences to appoint the French marshall Ferdinand Foch as overall commander to coordinate all Allied activities.[3] For the United States and the AEF it meant dramatic changes in training and operational plans, as Pershing had to send U.S. forces into the trenches sooner than anticipated. Furthermore, he had to abandon the AEF's training program as the Allies became desperate for soldiers. Over the next several months, "trained, partly trained, and eventually untrained soldiers were being shipped to France willy-nilly to meet the demand for replacements."[4]

The changing situation directly affected the 42nd Division and the other American forces in France. Pershing offered the Allies the service of the four AEF divisions that were closest to being fully trained—the 1st, 2nd, 26th, and 42nd divisions. Foch ordered these divisions to replace French forces in the quiet sectors so that the French units could be transferred to meet the German attacks (see map 2). The 42nd had begun withdrawing from the Lunéville sector to continue training elsewhere just before the Germans launched their attack. Its plans changed overnight, and Foch ordered the Rainbow soldiers to relieve the 128th French Division and to assume complete responsibility for defending the Baccarat sector. The new troops arrived on March 24, and the Rainbow officially took over the sector on April 1, becoming the first American division to have independent control over a sector of the front.[5]

The division's time in Lunéville and Baccarat was relatively peaceful, with the infantry rotating in and out of the trenches in eight-day cycles. They spent eight days in the forward trench, eight days in the reserve trench, and eight days in the rear.[6] Support troops were based behind the trenches and moved frequently to where they were needed. The soldiers generally experienced routine days of manning the trenches and carrying

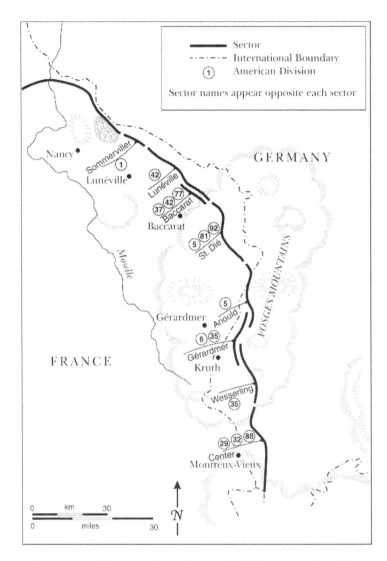

2. Areas around Baccarat where the 42nd Division was stationed in spring 1918. *Source:* American Battle Monuments Commission, *American Armies and Battlefields in Europe*, 422.

out support work. Nightly, the Americans and the Germans sent out patrols to reconnoiter enemy positions, capture prisoners, and/or examine the condition of their own wire and other defenses.[7]

Despite being relatively peaceful, these sectors provided a true

5. American soldiers in trenches. Courtesy of the General Douglas MacArthur Foundation.

eye-opener to the doughboys because they witnessed war's wholesale destruction for the first time. In Baccarat "irregular walls and piles of brick and stone were all that revealed where a school house, retail stores, and residences had once stood."[8] In addition to seeing this damage, Brownie and other American soldiers experienced limited combat for the first time, receiving intermittent artillery, machine gun, and rifle fire each day. They also experienced their first casualties.

MARCH 7, 1918

My dearest Marty,

It's a week last Sunday since I wrote you so I feel rather guilty, especially since I received a letter from you in the meantime. Shall I fall back on the old excuse that we have been very busy? Anyway I'll say that we work as hard as any of the other troops I have seen over here. . . .

I wonder when this war will end. I used to think I knew something about it but now I can't even guess. So many French soldiers have asked me that same thing and seemed to hang on the answer. Here one knows much less of the war than in the U.S. I never think much about it only in connection with something else which unino. . . .

I'll never mention your socks or mine—I mean the socks which are coming. I will say I wish I had them right now. They will be very, very welcome at any time Marty cause there is always more or less mud on the front. I can wear them in my boots. At present I've worn out all my socks but one pair, and don't know where more are coming from.

APRIL 17, 1918

. . . The mud is still very bad tho it looks as if we may have some better weather soon. This is sure a muddy country. If it were fair, it would be beautiful here. Seems as if every tree and bush were in blossom now but we can't enjoy it in the rain.

MAY 5, 1918

You asked me something about Bully-Beef. We don't call it that if it's what I think you mean. Corned-beef we call "Corned-Willie." We always call our emergency rations Corned Willie and Hard Tacks. That's what we have when everything else runs out. Corned Willie comes in a red tin box about a pound in each. Enough about Willie.

So you hear Ralph Clark is in the trenches.[9] They say we are in the same but it's not true exactly. We go in them to work or in front or in back of them, but don't make them our place of residence as the Dough Boys do. Engineers you know.

The trenches are funny things and it's not so bad there as some people think. If there is an attack or a raid then it *is* bad. Otherwise it's the safest place within five miles of the front. Just my opinion, tho. You don't have to keep your head up over the top for more than about five minutes tho, to start something. A machine gunner or a sniper might turn a few loose over your way. Another thing about trenches is how crooked they are. You never can tell where they go to, as you only see about twenty feet ahead. . . . Then there's no end to the wire entanglements. On all sides—an awful mess.

In the day-time there's not many men in sight. A few now and then. Most of them are in the dug-outs—asleep. Everything is very handy up there. Hand-grenades lying around in convenient places, all kinds of ammunition. Every little while a machine gun cuts-loose for a few shots or a shell passes over. There are duck-boards in all the trenches so you don't walk in the mud. My idea of the trenches, Marty, but perhaps not a very good one. Mostly we are about two miles behind them. A convenient range for all calibre shells and not so many holes to crawl into.

JUNE 15, 1918

Yesterday afternoon I went up to the front to finish up our work there. . . . Don't believe I ever told you very much about our sector. The part we worked in covers over a mile of front, and is all big woods. It is certainly surprising to get to the front line and then have someone tell you where you are. It looks like all the other trenches. There's no firing or very seldom any and the funniest part of all is the fact that there are no men. Sometimes you can go a half mile and not see one. It seems almost incredible but it's so. I tho't [I would] see a ditch and see men standing up shooting so it was a disappointment in a way. Of course men are there but they all sleep in the daytime except a few outposts and snipers. The woods are so thick that you can't see over two hundred feet while the enemy lines vary between 5 and 8 hundred yards. So a man can slip out easily enough—Snipers do it night . . . and we have had whole working parties out in no-man's land all day long. Of course there is barbed wire everywhere—in front, on both sides and in back. The lines don't move here as you can imagine the mess wire gets into after a couple of years. Now this is a "tranquil sector" so is perhaps not much like an active one. Sometimes for days we would only hear machine guns, an occasional sniper or outpost shooting, and the shells passing over. Then at night "gas alarm" & lots of artillery activity. The next morning some of our trenches shot up, and doughboys telling wild tales of what happened. Everyone of them saw Boches on all sides of him, when they were all in their dugouts asleep. [10] An Engineers viewpoint. Enough about war. . . . We'll forget there ever was a war someday. Will you?

Your Brownie will

Life for the 42nd Division in the Lunéville and Baccarat sectors revolved around activities in the trenches and dealing with natural elements that often made life miserable. Whether the soldiers were stationed in the trenches themselves or behind the lines in reserve positions, they were never more than a few miles from the front lines and almost always within artillery range. Brownie's regiment of engineers, for example, practiced digging trenches and studied trench warfare. The actual work of building and maintaining the trenches and other defensive positions was an endless task since they stretched more than four hundred miles from the English Channel to roughly the French-Swiss border. At the end of March, the 42nd Division was placed in charge of an approximately ten-mile stretch of the trenches. Generally, a trench system was constructed with a minimum of three roughly parallel lines of trenches called the front, support, and reserve. These trenches were connected in turn by communication trenches that permitted the movement of men outside the sight of the enemy. In front of the trenches the defenders strung barbed wire in layers, generally within fifty yards of their own positions.[11]

While the infantry obviously had the most risky jobs when it came to going over the top and launching an attack, engineers like Brownie often were in harm's way maintaining and expanding the trenches and wire entanglements. The engineers' really difficult job, one colonel wrote, "was to work repairing trenches and roads while under enemy fire."[12] Maj. William Johnson of the 117th Engineers explained:

> There are many odd fancies existing in this world of ours. One of them is that engineer troops wield only shovels, picks, saws and hammers. This fancy is entertained only by those who do not know or understand the difference between Army Engineers, Corps Engineers and Division Engineers during time of war. Actually, Division Engineer troops have to know their picks and shovels and their squads right and left as well. They have to know how to design and lay out a position for either offense or defense. They must . . . also know how to fight. They must know how to accompany tanks in attack (under fire the while) in order to cut barbed wire entanglements. And they must be men able to carry

everything infantrymen carry in addition to their engineer equipment. [13]

Simply living at the front compounded the difficult work. The men had even less chance to bathe; their diets remained limited to unappetizing rations; lice, rats, and other vermin thrived in the trenches and surrounding areas; and the rain and resulting mud made everyone miserable. No matter what rank, soldiers were louse infested when they came out of the trenches. [14] As one soldier recalled, "The dugouts and trenches were infested with body lice. These 'cooties' sucked your blood like ticks." [15] Rats were constant companions of the lice. A soldier, who served in the Baccarat area after the 42nd Division had moved on, described how "the rats abound and in the still of the night they sound like human beings—they are so big." [16]

The lice and rats flourished in part because the conditions in the trenches could not be improved. Latrine facilities were limited, and getting rid of trash was almost impossible. Furthermore, it rained almost constantly, producing a thick mud. "Never will the men of the 42nd Division forget the mud of Lorraine. Comrades may be forgotten, details of fighting go glimmering, marches and campaigns become hazy, but that awful February-March battle with the mud of Lorraine will stand out in their memories until final taps are sounded over the last surviving member of the division. For ten days the men . . . ate in mud, slept in mud, and dreamed of mud." [17] After a rain shower the mud was often ankle deep, and in a few cases thigh high. [18] An amateur soldier-poet captured it best in a poem entitled "Who Said Sunny France?" published in a May issue of *Stars and Stripes*:

It lies on your blankets and over your bed,
There's mud in the coffee, the slum, and the bread—Sunny France!
There's mud in your eyebrows, there's mud in your nose,
There's mud on your leggins to add to your woes,
The mud in your boots finds its place 'twixt' your toes—Sunny France!
Oh, the grimy mud, the slimy mud, the mud that makes you swear,
The cheesy mud, the greasy mud, that filters through your hair.
You sleep in mud, and drink it, that's true;
There's mud in the bacon, the rice and the stew,
When you open an egg, you'll find mud in it, too—Sunny France!
There's mud in the water, there's mud in the tea,

There's mud in your mess kit as thick as can be,
It sticks to your fingers like leaves to a tree—Sunny France!
Oh, the ruddy mud, the gliding mud, that sprays your pants and coats!
It cakes in your mouth till you feel like an ox.
It slips down your back and it rests in your sox,
You think you're walking on cut glass and rocks—Sunny France!
There's mud in your gas mask, there's mud in your hat,
There's mud in your helmet, there's mud on your gat,
Yet though muds all around us, we're happy at that—Sunny France!
Oh, the dark, dank mud, the rank, rank mud, there's just one guy to blame.
We'll wish him well (we will like H-ll!) and Kaiser Bill's his name![19]

While the mud, lice, and difficult work challenged the soldiers' health and endurance, the division's initiation to combat raised the stakes even higher.

MARCH 20, 1918

Dearest Marty,

I wish it would stay good weather tho, cause we start on a [censored] mile hike soon.[20] Hobo of America in France now Marty. As soon as it sprinkles here the mud gets up to one's neck, and it's four times harder to march when the road is "slick". That's an expression of S.C. [South Carolina] I think. You won't know me when I get back to the states, Marty. I say "Yonder," "You all," and other words foreign to me "before the war." . . .

It's surprising how cheerful the boys always are and what little things [censored] invent to amuse themselves. We have worked nights for a long time now and the tougher the weather the more cheerful the boys are. I think we are much happier than the French but as a rule they're older and have had four years of it. Some nights we have marched four miles with our rifles and [censored] worked six hours in the rain and snow putting up entanglements. Usually no gloves and our feet weighing fifty pounds apiece with sticky mud. Some nights we were shelled on top of all the rest, then marching back everyone is more cheerful than ever.

MAY 24, 1918

There's no news to speak of up here. Every day the same thing. We all wish we could start across and keep going right to Berlin but we must wait for orders. Someone else knows best and the war drags on. Every day we go to work with three Boche balloons looking at us.[21] They don't bother coming over to see us tho and seem quite harmless. I think they direct artillery fire and watch to see where we go and what we do if they can. We have them too and not far from the front. They can't be hit by shells cause they can be too easily raised or lowered or moved from one side the other. . . .

Brownie

While the soldiers endured these conditions, they "developed a routine of training, building and maintaining the trenches, and going out on an occasional patrol."[22] As the Rainbow moved to the Lunéville section in February, AEF headquarters estimated that the division would need one month training in the trenches and an additional month training in division formations before it would be ready to engage in combat in an active sector.[23] Therefore, training continued. Lt. Hugh Thompson recalled, "We practiced mock raids in an elaborate trench system with live bombs. Instructions followed with gas masks, chattering machine guns, Chauchat rifles and booming trench mortars."[24] The training generally went well, although the officers and soldiers made mistakes typical for men entering the trenches for the first time, including moving around too much and not staying hidden. They also had to deal with occasional equipment shortages.[25]

Brownie and the engineers built and maintained trenches, barbed wire entanglements, dugouts, roads, barracks, artillery and machine gun positions, and observation posts.[26] One engineer described the regiment's many roles: "They built dugouts in record time, they directed the digging of new trenches, and the repairs of old ones, they put in or repaired barbed wire entanglements in No Man's Land under the machine gun menace of the enemy. They ran sawmills and repaired roads under shell fire. They learned gas defense and how to dodge shells. They built bridges and light railways and barracks."[27]

The more mundane training and experiences did occasionally give way to more exciting and dangerous activities. The Germans fired an average of six hundred shells a day at Allied positions around Lunéville and Baccarat from the middle of February to the middle of June. Although these attacks were generally only harassing in nature and of little significance when compared to other bombardments the division later endured, they did raise the soldiers' risks and created more work. The obvious danger was that the soldiers sometimes had to work while under fire. [28] One doughboy wrote in March 1917 that "I cannot describe the sound of a shell traveling thru the air. It is a combination of a scream, a moan, a sigh and a screech." He added, "I thought I was going through hell on earth. Just waiting for a big shell to put you out of your misery. Just at present I am a nervous wreck, after four days and nights of bombarding, who wouldn't be." [29]

The attacks, even if limited in scale, could occasionally cause serious problems. "Raids and artillery action," one engineer wrote, "meant plenty of work for the engineers. Caved in trenches, badly damaged dugouts and improper drainage gave plenty to do during the day, leaving the night hours for the repairing of torn-up wire entanglements that had suffered from enemy fire." [30] This work, however, paled in comparison to the casualties. After one German barrage in early March, engineers frantically tried to dig out soldiers buried in the trenches and dugouts. What they found was horrifying: "Two of the boys had carefully removed the first body . . . . Then Harold Lorden and I got a litter ready, and we each grabbed hold of a leg to drag out the second fellow. We pulled, but the leg in Lorden's hands was not fastened to the poor devil's body, and Lorden went sprawling over backwards, the leg hitting him squarely in the face." [31]

The German artillery attack on March 7 caused the Americans much consternation, killing twenty-one officers and men and wounding another six. [32] The Rainbow's soldiers caught a gruesome glimpse of war's realities and realized that they had a long way to go before they would be ready for active combat. One of the French liaison officers to the division explained why the losses were so high: "The causes of this fire of destruction are not difficult to define. The American soldiers, like all troops who make their debuts in war, show themselves much too much." [33] This lesson was only one of many that the doughboys had to learn as they prepared for battle.

The artillery attacks revealed another area where the Americans were sadly deficient—gas warfare. Gas attacks had been used widely in the war, but the Americans were not prepared for them. The Rainbow soldiers, for reasons still unknown, struggled

6. Engineers from Brownie's 117th Engineers Regiment repairing
trenches in March 1918. Courtesy of the General Douglas MacArthur
Foundation.

to adapt to this form of warfare even after experiencing several
attacks and undergoing training. A leading historian of gas warfare in World War I notes that "the gas training and gas discipline
of the 42nd does not appear at any time to have been of particularly high caliber."[34] The belligerents used a variety of gases
during the war, including chlorine, chloropicrin, phosgene, tear,
and mustard.[35] Almost all of the gases attacked the eyes and
the lungs, while mustard gas "was chiefly effective as a painful
disabling agent. Wherever it touched moist skin it caused burns,

7. American soldiers preparing for a gas attack. Courtesy of the
General Douglas MacArthur Foundation.

particularly under the armpits, on the head sweating under your
helmet, and around the genitals."[36] The 42nd Division experienced numerous false, and several real, attacks in the spring
of 1918. The false alarms proved annoying because they usually
occurred at night.

The real attacks could be deadly, as when the Germans fired
more than four thousand phosgene and chlorine shells on May
27.[37] The attack began at 12:55 a.m. with "a terrific crash that . . .
rocked the entire sector . . . . Hundreds of bulking missiles, wob-
bling through the air with a sickening rush, exploded in their
midst, and terrified shouts of 'Gas!' warned them that they were
in for the greatest of horrors, a night gas attack."[38] The gruesome
scene was recalled by 1st Lt. John Taber: "The effects of the gas
were everywhere apparent. Everything was dead . . . . Messenger
pigeons lay in their baskets; rats, swollen and distended, were
stretched out in the trenches and dugouts . . . . The whole area
looked as if it had been visited by a killing frost."[39] The pigeons
and rats were the least of the victims: 37 men died in the attack
and another 160 were wounded.[40]

On other occasions, the 42nd Division experienced other
types of wartime realities because of its own choices. Nightly patrols across no-man's-land periodically engaged German forces.
On one occasion, the division commander decided to launch a

larger raid involving more than 350 men against the German positions. The division sent out these forces for several reasons, ranging from testing men in battle to gathering intelligence. On the larger raid and the patrols, infantry units provided most of the manpower, but other groups, like the engineers, also had active roles.

MARCH 20, 1918

Dearest Marty,

. . . I'm telling you all this now because our first month's training is over today. We came up to make trenches, dugouts and wire entanglements. We worked days till the Boches saw us and from then on nights. We knew very well when they saw us. I'll never forget the first shell I heard. It didn't strike very near but the sound of it nearly scared me to death. The second day we went out they dropped about 30 shells in and around our company during a period of 10 minutes. Didn't kill or wound one of us tho. The worst part of it is that you can hear them coming but don't know where they will strike. It always seems to me as if they had me picked out.

One gets accustomed to shells so that now we never pay much attention to them unless they strike closer than 500 feet. One night they sent four at us when I was in the middle of some entanglements. They hit so close as to throw dirt all over me where I was lying. Couldn't get away explains why I stayed. That is what they call a quiet sector but I can't understand where they get quiet from. There's always more or less artillery action, and they shoot on several airplanes every clear day. To see a shooting on airplanes is very beautiful. It's a clear sky and one hears a shell explode in the air. The sound of the gun and the sound of the explosion are both different so one can tell what's going on. You look way up in the air and see puffs of black and white smoke appearing, then looking closer you see the airplane. As the plane comes nearer you hear the rattling noise of machine guns. Nothing gets the airplane tho—they just can't seem to hit them, and the French planes are somewhere else. They did get a Boche last Sunday tho. He fell in flames. It seems funny to me that they can't hit an aviator especially as they shoot three and four inch shells at them.

One night the Boches raided a city near here and dropped bombs. The explosions of shells in air looked just like a lot of fireflys. The bombs they drop are very large and leave the machine two at a time, one from each wing, so as to hold the balance. They are usually both of the explosive and incendiary type. I don't believe any kind of shelter protects one from a large bomb.

Night before last the French batteries opened up all around where we were working. The Boches must have tried a raid. You can see the flashes of the hundreds of guns when they open up. Then you can hear the shells passing overhead with a sort of tearing sound. They don't sound half bad cause we know where they're going. Of course the answering fire isn't so nice. Then the star-shells and signal lights, and rockets. It sure is a mess on the front, Marty. The star shells burn for about three minutes & light up for a mile around.

Monday the Boches brought down a French observation balloon. Disguised one of their airplanes and the aviator shot into the balloon with a machine gun. The observer got out in his parachute but the balloon burned up.

This town is within easy range for shells but they never have hit it yet—not since 1914. It was partly burned then being taken by the Boches then retaken by the French. . . . Some shells are bursting might close now tho

APRIL 7, 1918

We had quite a scare here the other night. The gas alarm sounded but there was no gas. Might just as well have been tho, cause we were thinking the same things as we would have, had there been one. We were working in the night and horns and bells started sounding. My first experience, and it seemed like it was pretty risky—my life depending on that little mask. Tho't there might be some defect or something the matter. One can't see at all with them in the night and he can't talk or work and the clamp hurts his nose. All kinds of troubles mostly caused by imagination. A danger one can't see or hear is the worst. At best it was very oppressive the other night. All for nothing, too.

There's about as much news here as usual. Same old thing. Work-ing, eating and sleeping with a few shells occasionally for variety. A gas scare once in a while. You wake up about 3 a.m. and see some-one standing over you with a gas-mask. You never ask questions. Then you begin wishing that it's a false alarm and you remember all the stories about gas attacks that last two days. The clamp hurts your nose and you imagine there's fifty holes in the mask. Then someone says, "Masks off, false alarm." A great relief!

MAY 29, 1918

. . . Last night I quit work at eleven and then was kept up till two by gas alarms. Wish they would fight by day only. Perhaps I'll write a note to the Kaiser and request it. I expect to be up again tonight as the wind is in a bad quarter. This gas at night scares me as I sleep too sound to hear the alarm.

JUNE 3, 1918

. . . Of course when you get this letter you will have long since read the "official communiques" but I'll make my report just the same. Some airplane activity and artillery duels. Isn't that natural? In addition a "fake" gas alarm last night. I walked around for an hour in the night air peering thru my glasses & trying to find someone to tell me to take my mask off. . . .

Love,
Brownie

The engineers provided valuable assistance for patrols and raiding parties in several areas. First, they made maps of the areas targeted for attack and reconnaissance. Second, they built practice trenches for training, where the troops assigned to the missions then "practiced the raids several times daily for a cou-ple of weeks."[41] Finally, engineers often volunteered to go on the raids to demolish targets in the German lines. For a raid in early May 1918, more engineers, including Brownie, volun-teered than were needed.[42]

This particular raid occurred in the early morning hours of May 3 and was the largest one carried out by the 42nd Division in the Baccarat sector.[43] The raid's objective was "to take prisoners, to clean out and destroy the enemy works in the salient of Bois des Chiens."[44] More bluntly, Corp. Mannie Forte explained that the objects of the raid "were to penetrate to his third line about six or seven hundred yards, kill everything we saw, blow up his dugouts, take his machine guns and blow up their nests, and in other words demolish everything."[45] While the infantry went forward to eliminate any enemy opposition, the engineers followed close behind, each carrying twenty pounds of explosives to destroy German positions.[46] The raid was planned weeks in advance and involved close cooperation between artillery units, infantry, and engineers.

After training for the raid for more than two weeks, the raiding party of 21 officers and 346 men, including 29 engineers, left its preparation area at 11:30 p.m. on May 2 and arrived at the jumping-off point in the trenches around 3:15 a.m. on May 3.[47] There was a disquieting stillness in the trenches. The division's official historian remarked that "the men in the trenches in readiness were absolutely quiet and it seemed as though the whole world were at rest."[48] At 3:58 a.m. an American artillery barrage broke the silence. Over the next hour, the American field artillery fired more than sixteen thousand shells against the German positions.[49] Corporal Forte described how "the guns began with a deafening roar, shells were bursting all around us. . . . We went over in a fast walk and the shells were falling around us like pouring peas from a sack. You could not hear anything for the noise."[50]

The raiding party advanced under heavy artillery and machine gun fire before reaching its objectives.[51] The American artillery fire had been devastatingly effective—where the German trenches were supposed to be, the raiders found the forest "completely destroyed. Its trenches were filled, all works above ground leveled, wire entanglements torn down, and the forest itself turned into almost a bare field."[52] Forte wrote, "When we got over there you could not tell where the trenches had been. Everything was blown to pieces."[53] The official report of the raid explained, "the terrain in front of the enemy fire line for a depth of from 100 to 200 meters was found to be a field of shell holes."[54]

In the end the raid achieved the objective of destroying some German positions but failed in producing any prisoners. However, for the soldiers who experienced it, it was a memorable event. As one soldier who went on the raid recorded in his diary, "We had the feeling of veterans who had tasted the reality of war."[55]

APRIL 13, 1918

Marty dearest,

Of course I've seen some sad things, but as a rule the [French] people seem very contented. However, everyone is disgusted with the war. I can't see how France stands up under the war as well as she does. America I don't believe could sacrifice the things France has. I'll tell you many of the terrible things when I get back. No use making this letter blue by reciting them now. And still the war goes on. These Boches are Devils I guess.

So you want me to go "Over the Top" Marty. Perhaps I will if the war continues but I can't say I fancy it. Guess I'm afraid of machine-guns. We hear them from here and I hate the sound. We may have a chance to volunteer to go soon. Some engineers have gone. I'm waiting to see how I feel when the time comes to volunteer. Someway I don't feel very courageous when the shells start falling.

MAY 5, 1918

Found a letter from you waiting for me when I came in here last night. I've been away from home for about two weeks—not a vacation tho. . . .

I have a great yarn to tell you Marty but am not going to attempt it to-night. Not long ago I volunteered for dangerous work and was accepted. We went into training for about a week then went on a little raiding party. I was crazy to see just what going over the top would be like so had to try it once anyway.

MAY 12, 1918

It's a long week since I wrote you and in the meantime I've received two letters from you. Told you a week ago I'd write you a description of going over the top, but don't know whether I can now or not. I'll try if I get the right mood. Guess I'm getting moody lately. Fact is I would love to get back to Conn. to see a little good weather. Nearly three months of muddy France on the front has filled me up with longings. Can't say I want to quit, tho. I still want to see the end of this war. . . .

So the papers are full of tales about the poor Sammies. . . . For the past week I've been working up in the front line so I hear all the tales. It's not so very dangerous up there so long as you look out for snipers. It is very interesting. All kinds of ammunition, grenades, etc. lying around in convenient places. The thing that strikes me most up there is the amount of wire up in No-Man's Land. They must have worked at it for a good many nights. Not a nice job either. I've been working right around the spot where I went over but it's not quite so exciting as it once was. Now I'll try to tell you something about it.

Our raiding party arrived in the front line at about 3:15 a.m. We only marched about 2 miles the other part of the trip being made by auto truck. Our detachment of engineers carried only trench-knives and 45 Cal. Colts for defense. For demolition we carried about 20 lbs. of dynamite. Then of course our helmets and two gas-masks each. It was a starlight morning but rather misty. As we entered the first line there was practically no shelling but several machine guns in the rear kept up a steady fire. After getting into position we still had about a half hours wait as zero hour was 4 a.m. At 3:45 a.m. it commenced to get light a little and we all commenced to get a little cold and nervous. Someone kept saying 15 minutes more—10 mins. more—5 mins. more. Then our barrage started at 4 a.m. It seemed as if the air were full of shells and I wondered if they were all our own. Immediately the word came—"Out of the trench." It seemed impossible that we had to go out in such a Hell as was in front of us. It seemed as if the shells came from every direction at once as I think they did and thru all the pop-popping of machine guns. But we went. . . . We passed thru some willows thru gaps in two lines of wire entanglements then out into an open meadow or what was left of one and up a hill. Our barrage was striking half way up the hill and in the half dark it looked like a forest fire. It lifted as our first wave came up and went to another line nearer the Boche trenches. I remember feeling hot and choked, and drank water twice from my canteen. On the left I saw two large red balls of fire rising from the Boche trenches, and knew at once that it was a signal to their artillery for a counter barrage. We had been warned that no matter how bad their shell-fire we must go on. Looking at those signals nearly fixed me for I fell into a shell hole about five feet deep and with about two feet of water in it. Then we came to the edge of woods again where we had been taught the German front line was. I couldn't for the life of me find any trace of trenches. Nothing at all left of them. I have never seen such destruction before. The largest trees even 18 inches in diameter broken off anywhere from the ground up. And no ground left to walk on hardly. All we could do was walk along the edges of shell craters. Our barrage had shaped itself into a box shaped arrangement by then so we went on back toward the 3rd line trench looking for dug-outs to blow-up. We could see our bayonet men and machine-gunners running on ahead, so we followed. The smell of explosives was terrible. Our machine gunners soon had a perfect hail of bullets going down thru the bush. We found one dug-out near the edge of the barrage so near that every shell seemed like it would take my helmet off. The Boches started in with machine guns and shrapnel but not very heavy. They were throwing up star-shells also even in the day-light as it was then. There was nothing else to be gained so we started back across No-Man's Land. I wasn't sorry to go either. The American trenches looked good to me, but we went right to the rear. We were delayed for about a half hour there and the machine guns nearly drove us wild. We began to feel the effects of the raid then and all had head-aches. Finally we got away completely, and had a rest for three days. Now all of the fellows are waiting for another raid. . . . I'm glad I went—wouldn't have missed it for anything.

Things seem pretty stale since that morning—naturally! I must come to an end of this letter some time and I think about here. Tomorrow starts work again and we keep at [it] pretty steadily. We are willing tho, anything to win the war. Then Marty our turn will come—then. But good-night now Eve and write to you own.

Brownie

Brownie continued to show his love and commitment to Marty despite the numerous hardships he faced in the mud and gloom of northeastern France. The war, of course, posed serious challenges to Brownie and Marty's relationship. Brownie evidently did not write enough or did not respond as favorably on occasion as Marty would have liked, but their efforts to communicate did not fail. Their relationship strengthened through the trials of the spring of 1918 and persevered through even tougher times later in the war.

MARCH 11, 1918

My dearest Martha,

Has something happened to me or you or both of us? Last night came a letter from you of January 20th and about four days ago one of February 3rd. In both of them you seemed to doubt the welcome they'd receive. I don't know what makes you think that way but imagine it's something or some way I wrote you. I know I can't write the way I should, and that I don't write often enough. I simply can't get in the right mood, and know some of my letters must seem rather stiff or forced. But as for your letters being unwelcome really I live for nothing else than to read your letters and to get back to you some day. And still I can't write nice letters to you. It must be because of conditions and environment and those are something that no one in the U.S. can understand. I'm not kicking about our army as without doubt, it's the best treated one in the world but it's war over here and we are soldiers. . . . You're a wonderful girl, Marty and understand how to be cheerful and patient and I don't blame you a bit for wanting to know how welcome your letters are. . . .

If only you can wait till after the war—letting me write love letters when I can. I love you today almost too much. Must be the weather. It's not that—I love you always only its hard to tell about it in miserable weather when one is living in a barn and usually tired out from marching thru mud. . . .

I hate to keep thinking of you so as not to swear too much. Good-bye now Marty and try to love me even if I have a mean disposition. I'll love you always and forever in war and peace.

MARCH 20, 1918

It's nearly spring but how much different for us than the last one. Perhaps the next one will be better than all others. I've been feeling so cheerful and happy lately that I think the war must be going to end, tho perhaps that was caused by the weather. For two weeks it has been most beautiful and I received several letters from you. That's getting good things together. Now as I havn't had a letter from you for a week or so, last night I clouded up and commenced raining. See how you affect the weather! . . .

I'm going to send you some copies of "our paper"—the *Stars and Stripes*. It's fine and tells things *exactly* as they are. I don't know as you will enjoy it as much as I do but if you want to know just what the A.E.F. is, read the *Stars and Stripes*.

APRIL 3, 1918

. . . No mail at all for some time now, but I'm getting used to that. I know you write every week or oftener so sometimes I get a little sore when I have to wait two or three weeks. However Uncle Sam does pretty well for us, everything considered. . . .

How can you keep on loving me, Marty? It must be hard sometimes isn't it? . . . Surely we'll do all our nice things over again only it's sure to be much nicer. They're "memories" now but "realities" soon. But my memory is still good Marty. I have in it the best picture of the nicest girl. And the very little things we have done together come back so clearly sometimes. It hurts a little but still is the pleasantest thing on earth. . . . I think of you 100+ times a day so write to me. . . . You're the best sweetheart in the world and I'm your very own.

JUNE 15, 1918

. . . There's getting to be a little moon each night now. How many we have missed! Just think how much we'll have to make up. France is a non-romantic country. I even think sometimes when I look at the moon that it would be a good night to put up barbed wire. Sometimes I think of other things and other times. Uno Marty. We'll forget there ever was a war someday. Will you?

Your Brownie will

The 42nd Division soldiers passed their initiation to trench life and combat operations while in the Lunéville and Baccarat sectors. They gained invaluable training and a taste of the combat during their stay in northeastern France from February to mid-

June. They also learned some of the costs of war. One hundred and five soldiers died and almost one thousand were wounded while in these sectors.[56] The division took pride in being the first American unit to hold an independent sector in the trenches, and the men believed they were ready for more responsibilities. Those responsibilities would come in mid-July when the division began a period of almost four months of active combat against the Germans.

FOUR

Champagne and the Battle
of the Ourcq River

When the 42nd Division withdrew from the Baccarat sector in June, it was one of the most experienced AEF divisions. Only the 1st Division, which had launched a small offensive at Cantigny in late May, and the 2nd Division, which was becoming famous in the Belleau Wood, had more battle experience.[1] Upon withdrawal from Baccarat the 42nd was scheduled to be refitted and go through additional training. Then it joined the Champagne defensive and the Aisne-Marne offensive, and by the beginning of August the bloodied Rainbow veterans had emerged as one of the AEF's best divisions.[2]

The soldiers who survived the combat of late July and early August considered themselves lucky. The division suffered more than eight thousand casualties from July 5 to August 6 out of an initial strength of twenty-seven thousand.[3] Brownie revealed the thoughts of many when he wrote Marty, "The army is nothing nice in a place like this front has been. It makes a guy feel the uselessness of war when he sees men shot up and killed." While the division's service in Baccarat had provided a glimpse of war, the Champagne defensive and Aisne-Marne offensive introduced its full cruelty.

Dearest Marty,

I wonder where we were "a year ago" to-day. Times have changed for us all right but as long as we remember it helps some.

It seems a long-long time since I wrote you, and it is two weeks. I guess you'll wonder if I'm lost. We've been on one of our "tours" of France and when our post office hasn't been out of commission, I've been too tired to write. We've hiked and entrained and hiked again and are waiting orders to hike some more. Just now we're too near the front to have much fun and too far back to have any excitement. And I don't like the new section of France we're in. It's too flat and hot and uninteresting.[4]

It seems I'm fated not to write you Marty. Last Sun. eve. I started a letter but had to stop to arrange for a detail Mon. Well Mon. I left here at 6:30 a.m. in a truck and wasn't back in time to write before taps. This afternoon I started this one and as soon as I started we had to get out and drill. . . .

I don't believe we would mind your mother if we could go camping out again. I mean mind having her go—of course we wouldn't mind her. . . . Marty, I surely won't forget about writing on "our day." If I have to write hiking and have to use a newspaper margin. I'm going to write again before then tho—to make up for lost time. . . .

Nearly the 4th of July and I do remember that also, Marty. But the good days will come again Marty—Here's hoping. Do you know who loves you?

I must write you a few lines to-night. . . . Just think—the 4th has been gone a week tomorrow—but how long when you get this letter. Time goes by fast in the army. It hardly seems possible that I enlisted over a year ago.

There's been nothing very exciting going on around here lately. A pretty stiff bombardment just now on our front lines by the Boches. I just looked down there. It's ten-thirty P.M. and they're more than sending up signals. I expect our friends here in the grove will answer soon.[5] We still are in dog-tents & our French 120's are with us.[6] I wouldn't mind seeing the battery go as the

8. Gear carried by the average doughboy. Courtesy of the General Douglas MacArthur Foundation.

Boches may have it located. You may have heard of drum-fire. I think that's what is going on now. Almost a steady rumble. Probably a small trench raid as one of those make some fuss. Perhaps we'll have some peace after this bombardment stops. Last night I was kept awake all the time by the cold and the shooting. I havn't been going out night[s] as I've been working in the daytime at the office. It rained some last night and turned very cool and imagine my job keeping warm. One side of the tent is open and I had one blanket to roll up in. My bed fellow came in at 4 a.m. & made me colder yet. Finally I did get to sleep and as no one woke me up I slept till 9 o'clock. Of course no breakfast, but I didn't mind that. I'll bet I get up tomorrow, tho. . . . I'm sending lots of love to you Marty.

As ever your own
Brownie

Brownie and his comrades left Baccarat in the middle of June and moved to the region around Saint-Germain, having spent more time at the front than any other American division. In

9. Rainbow soldiers disembarking from train in late June 1918.
Courtesy of the General Douglas MacArthur Foundation.

preparation for a new Allied offensive, the division underwent training for two weeks at the platoon, company, and battalion levels with an "emphasis laid upon the combined use of the automatic rifle and the machine gun." Brownie's engineers were also "trained for combat as infantry."[7] Besides infantry training, all of the units were required to practice marching at least ten miles in different formations.

During the training period, the 117th Engineers became acclimated to their dual role as engineers and infantry. They continued engineer training while learning how to march as a division, deploy for and launch an attack, and carry out rearguard actions. Finally, to better coordinate the engineers and infantry, the 42nd Division's commander assigned one company of engineers to each infantry regiment while designating the rest as infantry reserves.[8]

JULY 20, 1918

Dearest Marty,

Guess it will be a long space between letters from the way things are going. Fact is I have no idea when I'll be able to mail this letter. Perhaps it will suffer the same fate as the last one I wrote you. That was last Sunday and the letter was lost along with my fountain pen and numerous other articles. That's nothing tho as I consider myself lucky to have been able to get back here at all. Now that sounds worse than things really were, but they were bad enough. At any rate we spent the worst part of the attack in a dug-out. There must have been 1000 men in the same dug-out and it was about 40 feet deep. After about 18 hours we went to take an intermediate position acting as Infantry. We expected the Boches to advance to our position but luckily for us they didn't. It was a sight to see the battle tho. There's no describing such a thing as the bombardment. It extended for miles to our rear. And airplanes. I never saw so many. There was lots of gas shells too, and right now I'm suffering the effects of one sniff of the stuff.

We are in the rear now enroute for some place—no one knows where. Our post office is out of business now but I'll mail this letter as soon as possible. No doubt you've read more details of the battle than I'll ever know. All we know here is that a battle is on and we have no idea of how big a one it is.

I've had no mail from you for a long time, Marty, but that doesn't worry me at all. It's somewhere—I know. I hear the French have started an offensive & are very successful so far. I only hope the good news continues & the Boches soon give in. . . . Must quit now Marty—Love & love too.

Brownie

The division's training was essentially at an end, as on July 1 it was ordered to move to the Champagne region and serve under the command of French general Henri Gourand as part of the French Twenty-first Corps, Fourth Army.[9] Although General Pershing had consistently opposed amalgamation, he had grown concerned in late June that French morale was declining precipitously and only the presence of American troops could improve the situation. While he planned for the creation of a true American army in August, he agreed to allow several American divisions to serve under French command in Champagne—the likely location of the next German offensive.[10]

The Champagne region of northeastern France is a flat low plain with soil composed principally of chalk, and the area had seen brutal battles in 1914. "As far as the eye could reach," one doughboy remembered, "the terrain was honeycombed by

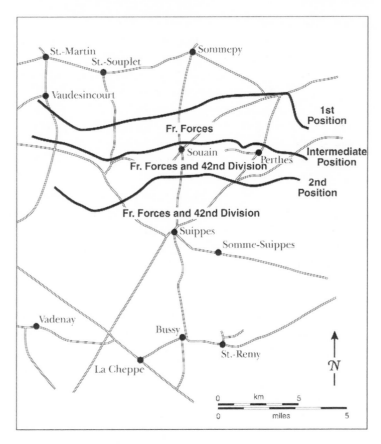

3. Position of the 42nd Division on July 16, 1918. *Source: United States Army in the World War*, vol. 5, 168.

a labyrinth of trenches hewn from the glaring chalk, and in the perspective it looked like a wrinkled old face."[11] The 42nd Division moved into new positions as the German army prepared for its final large-scale offensive of the war.

The key figure in the upcoming battle, Gen. Gourand, was one of the best French generals and a sight to behold. Brig. Gen. Douglas MacArthur, the chief of staff of the Rainbow Division, described the Gourand in his memoirs: "With one arm gone, and half a leg missing, with his red beard glittering in the sunlight, the jaunty rake of his cocked hat and the oratorical brilliance of his resonant voice, his impact was overwhelming."[12] Gourand had developed a plan to meet the anticipated German

10. Champagne battlefield on July 19, 1918. Courtesy of the General Douglas MacArthur Foundation.

attack by organizing an elastic defense with three distinct lines of trenches—forward, intermediate, and reserve. French volunteers, who were supposed to provide warning of the offensive and then slow the attackers, manned the first line. They realized that they were sacrificing themselves for the good of France. Approximately a mile and a half behind this first line was the intermediate position that was to serve as the main line of defense. The 42nd Division's infantry was placed here alongside French soldiers. A little more than two miles back was the second position containing reserve forces.[13]

The approximately twenty-seven thousand men of the 42nd Division joined four French divisions—the 13th, 43rd, 46th, and 170th—to form the 21st Corps. Gourand ordered the 42nd's infantry to occupy parts of the intermediate position and the 117th Engineers to serve as infantry reserves in the reserve position. By all indications, the French and American forces cooperated throughout the coming battle.[14]

Both natural and man-made obstacles marked the terrain. One Rainbow veteran wrote, "The Defenses in this section extended to a depth of five miles, consisting of concrete positions in the front lines backed by large masses of barbed wire behind which lay the second position."[15] A French general from the Fourth Army later explained that the terrain offered "the spectacle of the white lines of open trenches in chalk, the large craters of the mines, the interminable tangle of barbed wire hung about the trunks of the saplings. . . . During four years the adversaries had disputed each meter of this poor soil, and these struggles had left their traces on the terrain where the trenches intermingled in an inextricable network, where the barbed wire entanglements were in profession, joining the others."[16] In the two weeks prior to the German attack, Brownie and the other engineers improved the defensive positions.[17]

Gen. Gourand finalized his plans as the engineers completed their work on the defensive positions. Since the Allies had learned the basic German plans in the weeks preceding the attack from recently captured German prisoners, Gourand used the information to his advantage. He called for the greatest secrecy in hiding the Allies' knowledge of the German offensive design, for using a massive allied artillery bombardment as soon as enemy preparations for the attack were detected, and for the volunteers in the forward position to provide warning of the German attacks and to disrupt their advance as much as possible. He fully anticipated, however, that the intermediate position would be the center of resistance. In his instructions to his commanding officers, he asserted, "Beginning the moment the enemy strikes our intermediate Position, the fight really begins, and this Position should on the whole be the measure of the enemy advance. . . . THE ARMY IS THEREFORE TO WIN ITS BATTLE ON THE INTERMEDIATE POSITION."[18] An order followed these instructions permitting the use of force to prevent any unauthorized withdrawals.[19] His final admonition to the French and American soldiers was that "each shall have but one thought: to kill, to kill a-plenty, until they [the Germans] have had their fill."[20]

Nervous anticipation gripped the American soldiers as they entered the Champagne trenches. "The feeling that most impressed me," one soldier recalled, "was the light-hearted willingness which our force of American servicemen . . . anticipated the time when they would be called upon to play a definite part in perhaps the greatest engagement the world had ever known. . . . They asked only for the chance to win such a stupendous battle and save the day."[21] This indoctrination in battle began a little before midnight on July 14. The Germans planned to launch their attack with an artillery barrage followed by the infantry advance. The Allies learned the time of the offensive earlier in the day from some German prisoners. Gourand utilized this information to order a devastating artillery attack at 11:45 p.m. when the Germans had left their fortified positions in preparation for their assault. [22]

The Allied artillery bombardment caught the Germans by surprise. One German soldier wrote, "When they fire, it just hails, and we think every hour that our lives are at an end." Another one claimed, "The Americans are shooting with such effect that I am never sure of my life. . . . In this vicinity the Americans have been firing on us with one cannon after another so that we can't go out at all—what with shell explosions on all sides and men going down about you."[23] An American doughboy described how

> thousands of French guns broke the weeks of quiet and fired with an intensity that caused the atmosphere to shake with a constant rolling, unbroken sound. The deep roar of the heavy guns, smashing detonations of the middle calibers, and the bark of the 75's coalesced with the vibrating swishing note of the departing projectile. It was a hellish music. To its accompaniment, the stars were stuffed out and the skies turned in blotches and splashes and flashes to red, yellow and green. The surface of the earth was like a shaking table. [24]

Father Francis Duffy, a chaplain in the Rainbow, recalled, "No crescendo business about it. Just one sudden crash like an avalanche; but an avalanche that was to keep crashing for five hours. The whole sky seemed to be torn apart with sound."[25]

The Allied and German bombardments created a strange dichotomy of feelings: terror and entrancement. Pvt. Paul Bolin "thought hell had cut loose." [26] An American artilleryman explained, "I've never heard so much noise before, and don't ever expect to hear it again." He added, "It seemed as though the front for thirty miles each way had opened up and every gun was firing. It was as light as daytime, and the ground directly in front of us, and to the side of us, and behind us was a mass of flames and whistling steel from the bursting shells. The German drive was on." [27] Sergeant Elmer Straub exclaimed, "Every once in a while above the burst of the shells one could hear someone yell at a comrade or someone yell from a wound, but not a soul could be seen, nothing but the bursting of shells, the flash of rifles, the pep-pep-pep of machine guns and the general roar of the whole front."[28] A Rainbow soldier later captured the feelings that night poetically,

> Through that ghostly, ghastly silence came the midnight hour;
> And with it screams of death and hell, breaking near and far.
> Silence gave way to the cannon's angry roars;
> Still and thunder shattered Purgatory's doors.
> All hell broke loose and madly pounced upon the earth;
> The hour of Twelve, stroke of Twelve, and it was Horror's birth;
> Shrieking o'erhead missiles to maim and kill;
> Ablaze with angry flashes every road and hill.
> Trees were crashed to earth by flying steel that filled the air.
> Short was life for many who anger of the fiends must dare.
> Thus early hells raved on and many warriors died,
> Until night had passed and came the morning tide.[29]

The Germans launched their artillery barrage at midnight, and the night sky was quickly filled with the flashes of both enemy and allied firepower. The German high explosive and gas shells caused extensive casualties in the Allied lines. "There was death and destruction in the very air," wrote one soldier, "it seemed to be reaching out with hungry, clutching hands, sweeping victims in; the sky swished and swirled like a hurricane, bringing a rain that burst with a red crash when it landed, and the clean night breeze became a deadly draft of poisonous gas."[30] One officer reported, "A runner came staggering in [to the dugout] as though he was half dead. . . . He was gassed and in a bad condition. He told me this was the second time orders were sent to my position, the first two runners, Rodman and Bryson were killed. Rodman had his head blown off and Bryson the left foot while a piece of high explosive tore out his left side around the heart."[31] Rainbow veteran Henry Stansbury described how the barrage left one American soldier "dead in the road, gun in hand, his face scooped out as if done by a shovel."[32]

It was an unnerving experience even for those who were not wounded. First Lieutenant John Taber later explained that "one never conceived of such a thunder of sound. It was paralyzing, crushing." [33] An infantryman recalled, "The thud of the shells hitting in the vicinity jarred your ears every time one struck and exploded, and little streams of mud and loose pebbles would trickle through the cracks in the timber supports. . . . It was as hot as a furnace in the dugout for the entrance was closed with gas curtains and there was not a breath of fresh air." [34] "To think that I am still able to carry on, eat three meals a day and have a whole skin," wrote another soldier to his mother, "is to me nothing but a miracle." [35]

The Germans proceeded even though the Allies had anticipated their attack. Soon after 4:00 a.m. on July 15 the French volunteers in the forward trenches sent the message "Francois 570"—the code that the German infantry was advancing. [36] A major with the Rainbow wrote, "Wave after wave of Germans swept across no man land [sic] in close formation. They came over half of the distance without any marked break and then the French opened up on them with 75's [artillery pieces] that been placed for just that purpose." He added with a sense of horror and admiration, "The destruction was terrible and the advancing waves were torn and split apart. The great gaps [in the lines of soldiers] were filled, only to be again torn and shattered by the direct artillery fire. Doggedly they kept pushing forward . . . but the force of the charge was gone and they were beaten back." [37] A sergeant explained, "They advanced in mass formation and they were so thick you would shot [sic] at one and miss him and kill another. When they would get close to our trenches we would give them a few hand grenades and thin them out. . . . We had them stacked up in front of our wire two and three deep." [38] While the Germans were able to reach the intermediate positions, their initial efforts were ultimately stopped by 11:00 a.m. after hand-to-hand combat. [39]

The Germans renewed their efforts against the intermediate position on July 16. Despite launching at least seven different attacks between 8:00 a.m. and noon, they were stopped. [40] In essence, the Germans had lost this battle the first night, and by July 17 it was basically over. [41] A French general sent the following commendation to the divisions of the Fourth Army: "The German has clearly broken his sword on our lines. Whatever he may do in the future, he shall not pass." [42]

While some of the Rainbow soldiers had seen casualties in Baccarat, the Champagne defensive brought the war home full force. "Dead bodies were all around me," wrote one dough-boy, "Americans, French, Huns in all phases and positions of death. Shot in all vital places they sure presented horrible pictures. . . . It sure brings war & all its horrors home like nothing else could."[43] A lieutenant recalled how "the enemy continued to advance and through sheer numbers had succeeded in reaching the wire. Here the slaughter was terrible. The ground was covered with dead, while a boyau [sic] leading to the front was litterally [sic] choked with German bodies."[44] The 42nd Division's own casualties were even more alarming, as the attack left almost sixteen hundred men either dead or wounded.[45] Private Bolin remembered how he "could hear nothing but groans and moans from wounded men. I saw one shell explode, taking a comrade's head clean off is body. The body wriggled for a few seconds after."[46]

The experience of being wounded was horrifying. "All of a sudden bang," wrote one soldier, "& simultaneously I felt both arms go numb & my head felt like it had been hit with a rock. For just a second I was dazed & then blood poured down and filled my eyes."[47] Once wounded, a soldier faced a desperate struggle. There were insufficient corpsmen to bring him to the rear, and those men who made it there faced crowded and unsanitary conditions. "Hospitals were again swamped. Our field hospital with 200 beds," one doctor recalled, "was inundated by more than 3,000 wounded. . . . Men lay in the streets outside in the wet and cold; many who might have been saved died from exposure, shock, and lack of care."[48]

Those still in the trenches at the end of the battle witnessed destruction all around them. "During this time the weather was exceedingly hot, unburied bodies, and thousands of dead horses covered the ground. Everybody was dirty and baths an impossibility."[49] Another soldier lamented, "The wet and rotting sandbags of burlap had a pungent, unpleasant odor. The stench of latrines was pervasive and the effect of a high explosive (HE) shell making a direct impact on a company latrine can be imagined. The most sickening of all was the odor of putrid corpses in the hot sun."[50] Sgt. Tom Witworth explained that two days after the start of the German attack in Champagne, "The odor [from the dead] was something fierce. We had to put on our gas masks to keep from getting sick."[51]

The 42nd received orders on July 20 to withdraw from Champagne and prepare for a movement to another location.[52] As the soldiers moved, they could take solace that they had made a lasting impression on their allies and enemies. After the battle, German prisoners claimed they were fighting the "two best divisions in the American Army—the 42nd Division and the Rainbow Division."[53] A French liaison officer assigned to the 42nd asserted, "The conduct of the American troops has been perfect and has been greatly admired by French officers and men. Calm and perfect bearing under fire, endurance of fatigue and privations, tenacity in defense, eagerness in counterattack, willingness to engage in hand-to-hand fighting—such are the qualities that have been reported to me by all the French officers I have seen."[54]

The 42nd's doughboys left Champagne expecting to receive much-needed rest, but within days they were ordered to participate in their first major attack. Starting on July 18 other Allied divisions had launched the Aisne-Marne offensive. The attack was a new experience for most American forces, since prior to this point in the war only a few U.S. divisions had participated in major combat operations. Although still not fully trained, the AEF fought alongside the British and the French. After being temporarily moved to an area near Château-Thierry to serve as a reserve force for the American 1st Army Corps, Brownie and the rest of the 42nd Division were about to embark on their most bloody attack of the war.[55]

JULY 30, 1918

Dearest Marty,

Two letters from you yesterday and I was very glad for them. Tho I've not written you in a long time, I'm sure you'll forgive me when you understand the circumstances. This is the first time we could mail letters for nearly three weeks so I'm sending along another letter of a week or so ago.

This is not going to be very lengthy as I'm not exactly in the mood for writing. I'm going to wait till later, perhaps after the war, to tell you all of the experiences we've had just now. I want you to know I'm still O.K. . . .

This is all for now, Marty, but I'm sending lots of love to you.

AUGUST 8, 1918

Another letter to you after a long silence on my part. My letters from you come all right tho usually bunched. Now some excuses for not writing sooner or is that unnecessary? Anyway I'll tell you something about the recent events "here abouts". We have been on the front & would be now only the Boches went off and left us here. . . .

The army is nothing nice in a place like this front has been. It makes a guy feel the uselessness of war when he sees men shot up and killed. It's no use trying to describe it and I wouldn't want to. But now about "us Engineers"—we did go after the Boches one day acting as Infantry, and had the wonderful luck to advance 6 or 7 miles. Now the truth is there wasn't much scrapping tho we did shoot some and were fired on by both machine guns and artillery. The Boches were retreating and we were trying to worry and hurry them a little. We commenced our advance at 4 a.m. so hadn't slept any on account of hiking to the front. After the advance we slept in the wet and cold without blankets after a rainy day. I shall always think tho that perhaps that rainy weather saved some of us our lives. The next morning we were relieved and hiked back to camp and *Slept* some. Now my squad is on K.P. for a week and the front is far from us. Enough about the war. . . .

Your own
Brownie

The 42nd Division participated in the Aisne-Marne offensive from July 25 to August 3. On July 23 the division received orders to be ready to relieve the French 167th Infantry Division and the American 26th Division. The 117th Engineers arrived first with orders to prepare the area for the rest of the division's arrival. The 42nd traveled the night of July 24 and joined the 1st Army Corps, under the command of Gen. Hunter Liggett, and the 6th French Army, under the command of Gen. Jean Degoutte.[56]

The trip to the front was quite difficult and sobering. A medic in the Rainbow's 167th Infantry Regiment explained, "It is hard for people who merely study maps after a battle to understand how difficult it is to find one's way over unknown terrain, in the rain and dark, with no signs even when there are roads."[57] The conditions at the front were appalling. The American 26th Division controlled this part of the front prior to being relieved by the Rainbow. A private in the 26th recalled that, "the dead were so numerous, it was impossible to bury them for some time. The engineers combed through the wheatfields [*sic*], and when bodies were located, rifles were stuck in the ground in an inverted position with the butt sticking up over the wheat. Standing on elevated ground, thousands of these rifles could be seen, grim sentinels watching over the dead."[58] Another doughboy wrote that he "saw rows of wounded boys just brought in. . . . I probably saw a thousand or more of our American soldiers with every conceivable kind of wound—some with legs or arms blown away, some with eyes shot out, many with chins gone, others with every muscle in their bodies shaking as with palsy, shell-shocked, some with bodies burned by gas so badly that they were black."[59]

The 42nd Division trekked into this nightmare on July 24 and 25. One Rainbow veteran later wrote, "Along the outskirts of the village, toward Château-Thierry lay many more soldiers, and among them were some in khaki, American soldiers who had died while storming the hills to the east and breaking up the German machine gun nests in extending across the line of advance."[60] A corporal recorded in his diary that "the odor of dead things permeates the atmosphere everywhere."[61] As one sergeant advanced, he saw that "many, many dead Germans were lying about; some of them only blue skin stretched over bones and others only half buried having been uncovered by bursting shells. As we went through Vaux I saw several graves, some with a foot sticking out, and others with even the heads sticking out; they seemed to have been thrown in these graves any way and in an awful hurry."[62]

Even before beginning to fight, the division's men suffered because "the sanitary conditions on this front were as bad as possible—dead men, and horses being all around, unfilled latrines used by the Germans everywhere—Diarrhea became quite general in the entire battalion caused from having to drink the water from shell holes."[63] Still, even in their weakened condition, the soldiers assumed their new positions with optimism and the desire to fight the Germans outside the trenches.[64]

The Germans greeted the Rainbow on July 25 with a terrifying artillery barrage. Corp. Norman Summers remembered, "German shells, high explosives were bursting all around us and it was pitiful to see the sights." He added, "Some of our men were blown to pieces. Some had their legs or arms blown into tatters. Dead horses were lying everywhere and the stench was awful. Dead Americans, French, and Germans were lying everywhere."[65] A soldier in the division being relieved by the 42nd described that "as we sat side by side in my foxhole . . . a German shell screamed down close beside us, hitting a shelter tent where two men had been sleeping. To our horror, we saw one man blown high in the air, his body going asunder as he fell."[66] The artillery barrage eventually gave way to quiet as the Rainbow's infantry prepared for an attack the next morning.

The division's objective the next day was the Croix Rouge Farm where several hundred Germans, possessing more than thirty machine guns, manned strong defensive positions.[67] Lt. Edmund Hackett recalled that from the enemy's "several commanding positions a veritable rain of machine gun fire swept the woods in all directions."[68] The three thousand infantry in the attacking force paid dearly for its inexperience in offensive operations. American officers, blowing whistles and shouting to get their men into attack position, unintentionally alerted the Germans to the impending attack. The Germans reacted with an artillery barrage, "which fell with great violence upon the men while they were forming to start. Consequently due to the confusion, Companies jumped off through the thick woods minus platoons and in fact before going far the largest unit with any liaison was at the most two of those platoons acting together. It was for this reason that the fight soon developed into a platoon leader's war."[69] A lieutenant described in horror how "the hun barrage got us after we had taken ten steps forward in the advance. Ten minutes after it started the two platoons had been reduced to fourteen men and myself [out of forty-four]."[70]

As the infantry moved forward, one platoon after another was mowed down. A doughboy later wrote, "Line after line of the Alabamians . . . hurled itself against that position, only to waste away under the fountain of death."[71] The screams and moans of the wounded and dying reverberated across the fields. While the division ultimately captured the farm, it suffered heavy losses from machine gun fire and hand-to-hand combat.[72] The commander of one of the infantry regiments reported finding 283 dead Germans the next day with bayonet wounds.[73]

German defenders inflicted 800 casualties in the first two days of the battle.[74] Corp. Elmer Sherwood "stumbled over an American, one of whose legs had been blown fifty feet away. Beside him lay a German with half his face gone, black now, maggots pouring from the wounds."[75] Another wounded doughboy, after being evacuated to a hospital, saw another American nearby "with his head bandaged all over. . . . I could tell he had about fought his last battle by the way he breathed. His breathes came in short, quick gasps and with each breath the bandage on his head would get a little redder. . . . This boy, as he was getting those last breaths, would move the slightest bit as if it enabled him to breathe better—he was too weak to move much. . . . Then he was no longer in the army."[76]

The casualties endured pain from the moment of their injury throughout their stay in the hospital. As the fighting grew more intense in late July, there were often not enough stretcher-bearers to carry the wounded, resulting in "an almost continuous line of maimed men walking, crawling, staggering along the road" to the aid stations and hospitals. Even those who made it to the hospital faced considerable danger. Corp. Frederick Pottle described the typical morning routine at an evacuation hospital:

> Soon after breakfast the surgeon appeared and the dreadful ordeal of dressing the wounds began. The nurse accompanied him from cot to cot. . . . The orderly would cut the bandages and lay bare the great wound. The surgeon, equipped with sterilized gown and gloves, would pull out the old packing and tubes, often having to probe deep with the points of his instrument. Then he would swab it out with a gauze sponge soaked in Dakin solution, push new tubes and gauze back into it. . . . All this caused the patient excruciating agony.[77]

The Germans retreated the day after the battle of Croix Rouge Farm to defensive positions north of the Ourcq River under orders to retire slowly and inflict as many casualties as possible in the process.[78] Their defenses on the Ourcq "were naturally strong and skillfully arranged so as to command every approach, at the same time affording themselves almost perfect concealment."[79] Little fighting occurred on July 27 except when elements of the Rainbow approached the Ourcq's bank. That night the doughboys contemplated their first river crossing as the Germans prepared for the attack that they knew was coming the next day.[80]

The 42nd Division had to ford the Ourcq to reach the Germans. The actual width and depth of the river at the time of the attack has been subject to some debate. A report given to the division in the days preceding the attack claimed that the river was approximately 20 feet wide and 18 inches deep. However, accounts from the men on the ground claimed it was up to 60 feet wide and 12 feet deep. More than likely it was closer to the original estimate although swollen to a degree by rain.[81] Whatever its size, Brownie's engineers were responsible for maintaining existing bridges and building new ones, enabling the infantry to cross the river and continue receiving supplies.[82] The engineers led the way during the ensuing attack and ended up building two bridges over the river despite facing well-hidden snipers and machine gunners who hindered their work but could not stop them.[83] One of the YMCA workers assigned to the Rainbow Division described the engineers' work as "marvelous."[84]

The division received its orders on July 27 to spearhead the Allied attack before dawn the next morning.[85] Its mission was clear: "to push forward, seize crossings over the Ourcq and establish itself on the slopes to the north of the river."[86] Once across the river, the division was supposed to capture three key villages: Villers-sur-Fère, Sergy, and Seringes-et-Nesles, as well as the surrounding farms.[87] Surprisingly, the attack order emphasized that the soldiers were only to use their bayonets.[88]

Close hand-to-hand combat and a high number of casualties marked July 28. "The day was one of very fierce infantry fighting. . . . The enemy attempted to hold the line of the OURCQ and counterattacked us in force, but we succeeded in crossing."[89] A German lieutenant facing the attack described how "many of the enemy fell but others took their places. It was like killing a few bees from a swarm."[90] An American artillery observer explained that "in the yellow wheatfields [*sic*] on the slopes beyond the Ourcq the infantrymen from New York, Ohio, Iowa, and Alabama were busily at work. Sometimes they advanced through the fields in a single-line, crawling on hands and knees. Again they walked slowly abreast, occasionally dropping to the ground as if in response to an order, then rising and pushing ahead! There were times when some of those who dropped did not rise again, but lay still in the midst of the wheat."[91]

The Germans resisted with machine gun and rifle fire and launched an artillery barrage against the attacking forces. One soldier who survived the shelling exclaimed that the shells "made a hole in that wheat field large enough to bury a horse in. One was a direct hit on the terrace in our position. Blew three men at one *gun* into small parts, the largest part of a torso found was a thigh."[92] First Lieutenant John Taber later explained,

> Never was there a more vivid picture of the dreadfulness and brutality of war. Dead bodies, pitifully strewn about in grotesque attitudes of supplication, surprise, despair; some pitched forward on their faces, others crumpled up on their knees as death had caught them trying to struggle to their feet; some in repose, as if asleep; one or two still clenching in lifeless fingers, lifeless cigarettes; a few unrecognizable. Shells falling on men already dead. Everywhere, the debris of battle; here a blood-soaked shoe, there a pierced helmet; raveled puttees, dented canteens, torn blankets, gory litters. Not a pleasant sight to view, horrible to remember.[93]

The division renewed its attack north of the Ourcq on July 29 and fighting centered on Meurcy Farm. The Germans fought tenaciously from well-prepared machine gun positions.[94] A second lieutenant reported, "The position of the machine guns and snipers firing on the village seemed to be constantly changing, so that the infantry had great difficulty in locating any of them. The casualties inflicted on the battalion by this artillery and machine gun fire was heavy."[95] Brig. Gen. Douglas MacArthur claimed "the enemy machine guns are playing a very important part in the present battle. His gunners are in the grain fields along the ridges north of the Ourcq and keep up a constant fire on our lines. . . . Meurcy Farm was well defended with machine guns and was not taken until the gunners had been killed in hand to hand conflict with our men." [96] In his memoirs, MacArthur described how the men crawled "forward in twos and threes against each stubborn nest of enemy guns" and "closed in with the bayonet and the hand grenade. It was savage, there was no quarter asked or given." [97]

Over the next two days the doughboys continued to experience hard fighting. [98] On July 29 the Germans "made strong efforts to force us back beyond the Ourcq" and shelled the river valley "with high explosives and gas." [99] The combat was brutal— "Here a man went hurling into the air to fall to earth a shapeless, quivering mass; there another swirled completely around by the impact of a bullet full in the body." [100] Through it all the American soldiers were ordered "to grip the enemy all along the front and preserve close contact with him." [101]

Beginning on August 1 the Germans started to withdraw to positions beyond the Vesle River, and the 117th Engineers took center stage. Other than the engineers who had been responsible for the bridges over the Ourcq, the remainder of the regiment had been maintaining and building roads and serving as infantry reserves. Companies A and B, 117th Engineers, received orders on August 1 to act as infantry beginning the next morning. [102] This was the moment many of the engineers had been waiting for. The division's official historian wrote that "the 117th Engineers, who for the preceding days of the battle were disgusted that there was no use for them as an infantry reserve, were off to the attack like a shot. They were anxious to show the rest of the Division that engineers might build bridges and roads, but that they were also good infantry soldiers." [103]

As the Germans withdrew, the engineers stayed "on the heels of the Huns" throughout the next day and night. They advanced from five hundred to a thousand yards at a time, and then they "would dig little holes just large enough for one man to get in to keep from being killed by the heavy shells and machine guns." [104] These engineers advanced farther than any other unit in the division before they were relieved on August 3. The relief of the 117th represented the end of the fighting for most of the 42nd Division. After eight days in combat the division had advanced more than ten miles and forced the Germans to abandon extensive prepared positions.[105]

The division was exhausted after more than a week on the offensive and the several days of fighting in Champagne. The soldiers began to take stock of their losses on August 3, but no one was prepared for the numbers. Immediately after the battle the division reported 696 dead, 4,240 wounded, and 578 missing. The division's chief surgeon calculated that at least 6,400 casualties from the 42nd and other units had passed through his hospitals.[106] After all of the casualty figures were collected, the division's final tally was 6,459 dead, wounded, and missing.[107]

News of the battle and its casualties quickly reached the home front. The headline in the *Charleston News and Courier* on July 30, 1918, read, "River Ourcq Runs Red with Blood Where Americans Triumph Over Prussian Guard."[108] *Stars and Stripes* claimed, "the Ourcq has taken its place in the pages of American history as another Antietam."[109] The comparisons were apt. "The dead Americans and Germans were lying everywhere in the yards and fields."[110] A private recalled years later that he "was the only one in my squad of eight men that walked out of the battle."[111] "I have seen," one sergeant wrote in his diary, "more dead Americans in this little time than I ever did before in all my life and the smell was so bad that nearly all of the men put handkerchiefs over their faces."[112] John Brenner, another Rainbow veteran, recalled coming across "one man, who was on his knees, in a shell hole, his hands were on the gun in position to fire, a shell hit a few feet in front of him causing his head to be blown off and leaving him in this position."[113] He concluded, "One cannot believe the misery a person is in when they walk around seeing bodies everywhere and then realizing you may be one of them anytime."[114]

As the 42nd moved to a recuperation area, its men had time to reflect on their recent experiences. The division had earned the respect of its peers and opponents after the fighting in Champagne and in the Aisne-Marne offensive. Although it had suffered severely and needed both rest and replacement soldiers, the division was now battle hardened and considered one of the best in the AEF. However, special responsibilities came with such a reputation, and the division had not rested long before it began to move to participate in the First American Army's initial attack of the war.[115]

FIVE

Rest and the Battle of Saint-Mihiel

The battle of the Ourcq River had a profound impact on the 42nd Division. Nearly 20 percent of its soldiers had been either wounded or killed, and the survivors believed they had earned a lengthy respite from the war. It was not to be. After resting and recuperating a short time, the division was again on the move to participate in the first full-fledged American offensive of the war. General Pershing selected the Rainbow and several of the other most experienced divisions to spearhead the American assault on the Saint-Mihiel salient.[1]

Brownie had come through the preceding battle unscathed beyond the psychological shock of the carnage. As one of the Rainbow officer's reported, "the men had used up the last bit of energy they possessed." He added that they had "stood a tremendous physical strain—nine days of intermittent hand-to-hand fighting, coupled with excessive shell fire, much of which consisted of gas. Those nine days will also be long remembered, because at most the men received only one meal a day, and some days they had nothing to eat."[2] Brownie and the other soldiers believed they needed an extended rest period; they received ten days near the small village of Bourmont between the larger towns of Neufchâteau and Chaumont.[3]

Dearest Marty,

. . . Even soldiers rest sometimes—that's what we're doing now. . . .

This is such a nice quiet place. I've had time to get natural and wonder what's going on and think about things in general. This is our second day of rest and I wish you could see our camp, it's in such a pretty spot. We are camped out in an orchard. The country is hilly and wooded considerably. The orchard we are in is on a hill overlooking a French village. The weather is beautiful only very hot in the day time. Another kick—there's no fruit in the orchard.

And rest—we drill one hour, clean up some and then lie around and sleep and read all day long. About twenty of the boys from our Company went to Paris on a 48 hour pass last night. I was away when the order came so didn't even put in for a pass. However I'll go yet if I can. . . .

The boys have come back from Paris and I've been entertained by their yarns. No more passes are to be issued at present evidently and I'm much disappointed. Perhaps that means we leave here soon. In the Red Cross Restraunts in Paris the boys say one (a soldier) pays 3 sous for all he can eat. And a room for four francs a day at the Y. All that in expensive France. . . .

SEPTEMBER 1, 1918

I guess by this time or by the time you get this letter you'll have stopped looking for mail from me. And as usual I've no good excuse for not writing. I am getting like lots of the others. It gets harder and harder to write as time goes by. And there has been nothing special to write about—just camping around France waiting for something to happen. Once in a while a hike and some new scenery and a new town to look at. But even that gets tiresome. There is always too many soldiers around for one to buy what he wants from the civilians. Always a crowd. I'd like to go somewhere and not see an American soldier for two months. We are supposed to have a seven days leave but I think the hope is in vain. It looks that way now.

At present we are near quite a large town so we are hoping to

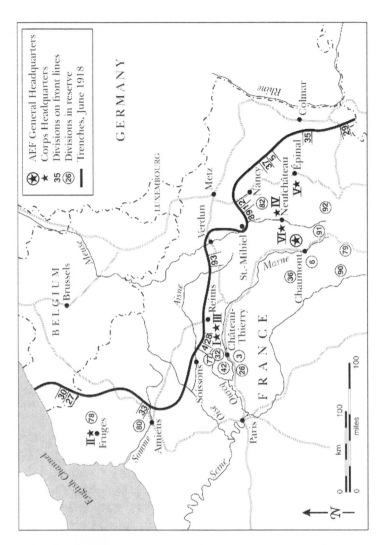

4. Location of American corps and divisions after the battle of the
Ourcq in early August 1918. *Source: United States Army in the World War,*
vol. 9, 5.

stay here awhile. There are entertainments and moving pictures for us nearly every night but I havn't attended. The crowd again. We aren't doing anything, tho so have all our time to wander around and sleep. We have baseball games all the while, too. All thru this section there are lots and lots of little white plums, sweet too. The only thing I ever saw that there was enough of for the army. I did manage to buy some chocolates yesterday at our canteen. The first I've ever been able to buy in France. We can buy about everything that's necessary over here, tho, and that's some improvement over last winter.

Perhaps I've become so tough in the army that you wouldn't want to talk to me. I know you would but I seem too different. . . .

From your own,
Brownie

Everything had to be cleaned and deloused after leaving the front lines. Many soldiers took their first baths since before the Germans initiated their July 15 offensive. The soldiers' wool uniforms were washed and redistributed, and clean socks and underwear were also made available. They also enjoyed their first formal entertainment in months when renowned entertainer Elsie Janis gave them a concert.[4] Some lucky doughboys received passes to Paris and other locales.[5] Brownie was not among them; so he had to content himself with the relaxed work schedule, beautiful scenery, and swims in the local streams.

One of a soldier's first priorities when he got away from the front lines was to eliminate "cooties." The AEF developed a standard system to delouse the soldiers. The soldiers placed their valuables in a numbered bag, stripped and put their clothing in another bag, and then placed the clothing in a large boiler. The clothing was free of nits and lice after about thirty minutes.[6] One soldier described the relief after donning his clean uniform: "For a few hours I won't have a cootie—how glorious!"[7] A lieutenant remarked that "everyone leaves the delousing station feeling like a new man—a little lonesome, perhaps, for the lost cooties, but happier and decidedly cleaner. It is a great sensation to be really clean after having been really dirty."[8]

Another task besides resting and cleaning was the integration of replacement soldiers into the division. While it had received new soldiers before, the division had never had to replace a fifth of its number. The difficulties were immense. The replacements needed training in their assigned roles and they had to acclimate themselves to well-established units. Unfortunately, the new men had received little training in the United States. "Many of them," one lieutenant later wrote, "were unable to read, write, or speak English; and, more than that, most of them had never fired a rifle." [9] Furthermore, the few who had some preparation had been trained with little regard for the realities of trench warfare on the western front. [10]

Pershing and his headquarters staff were busily planning the first major American offensive of the war while the Rainbow division was resting and recuperating. The American units that had thus far seen combat had been assigned to British and French armies and had served under their commanders. Pershing had assumed from his initial appointment as the AEF commander that as soon as the United States had sufficient forces in France to operate an independent army it would. That time came when Allied commander, Gen. Ferdinand Foch, authorized the creation of the First American Army in the summer of 1918. It officially came into being in August with Pershing as its first commander. [11]

The First American Army's initial objective was to destroy the Saint-Mihiel salient, which had protruded into the Allied lines since the early battles of the war. [12] While neither side had staged a major offensive there since the opening stages of the war, the territory offered potential opportunities for both sides. It presented the Germans an excellent location to launch an attack into northeastern France. For the Allies, Saint-Mihiel offered the opportunity to attack the flanks of the German forces and pinch off the salient. Both sides recognized the offensive possibilities but decided to build strong defensive positions and pursue major operations elsewhere. For almost four years, the Germans and the French used the Saint-Mihiel area as a location to rest troops before sending them to more active fronts.

The fact that this area was a quiet sector of the front and was close to the sector assigned to U.S. forces for training made it an ideal target for an American offensive. Soon after the first AEF troops arrived in France, Pershing and his staff viewed the Saint-Mihiel salient as the most logical location for the First American Army to launch its initial attack of the war. [13] Pershing wanted to launch an offensive that would prove the worth and capabilities of his forces. Failure was not an option he wished to contemplate. Saint-Mihiel offered a lightly defended area that American forces could attack while not venturing far from their supply lines and training areas.

The attack plan called for American divisions, with the help of some French units, to strike on both sides of the salient causing the German forces to either retreat or surrender. The terrain in the salient consisted of some marsh in the center, some woods, and a line of low hills. Pershing was determined to succeed and assigned his most experienced divisions to lead the offensive. The 1st and 89th Divisions, along with the 42nd, were scheduled to spearhead the assault. [14]

SEPTEMBER 21, 1918

Dearest Marty,

. . . You may think that there's nothing going on over here but we have had some excitement lately. We went thru a big attack last week in which I had a small part. Enough to get a good view of everything at least. Most of the platoon went over the top ahead of the dough-boys to cut barbed wire but I was unlucky or lucky enough not to go ahead. Anyway the reserves were not too far behind to see a little excitement. [15] It's a thing worth getting wounded for to see an attack like that. We were very successful, you know how much so. Now I'm living in the woods this time not in a dog-tent. We captured a lot of tarpaper so some of us made huts and I have a dandy one. Lots of room and warm and dry. Plenty of captured blankets and shelter tents to keep us warm too. In lots of ways the front is the better place to be in France. One can pick up almost anything he ever saw during an attack, but soldiers won't take much stuff on account of having it to carry. This is the second time this summer that we have been where we could get all kinds of Boche stuff but I never take a thing. There are lots of us who are not souvenir hunters. I'll think to take myself back from here will be enough of a souvenir. Anyway I wouldn't cry if I couldn't remember this place. . . . I must stop writing now Marty but here's a good-night and love.

From your,

Brownie

AEF headquarters assigned the 42nd Division to the IV Army Corps, First American Army, and gave it responsibility for a two-mile-wide sector of the front.[16] To maintain secrecy the division marched six nights and moved more than sixty miles to reach Saint-Mihiel in time for the attack (see map 5). The marches were extremely difficult and dominated by widespread confusion.[17] One Rainbow veteran griped, "Now I know why they call us the A.E.F. It means 'Ass End First.' "[18] It was cold and rainy on the marches, and the men were prohibited from smoking. "For days the rain has been pouring down. . . . Water! Water! Water!," another veteran complained. "It runs, it trickles, it oozes from everything, everywhere. The long column of infantry had been on the march for five black, miserable nights, drenched to the skin, splashing, squashing its way through the heavy liquid mud, . . . The men's blankets and packs are very heavy and soggy with water, their clumsy shoes like saturated sponges, their leggings plastered and caked with mud."[19]

The night the Rainbow's soldiers arrived behind the front lines was particularly bad. The diarist for the division's signal battalion wrote, "It was a pitch-black night, with a steady rain falling, and the mud was ankle deep. The roads were congested with traffic, and progress was well-nigh impossible."[20] Father Duffy remembered that men "moved to the jump-off point on the night of September 11th. The rain was falling in torrents. The roads were like a swamp and the night was so dark that a man could not see the one in front of him."[21] The German troops offered similar complaints: "We are full of mud and wet through," groused one German grenadier. Another German soldier wrote home, "Has the weather been as bad at home as here? For here it rains day in and day out. We are lying outdoors here under the open heavens. We never get dry and the things we have on our bodies will certainly rot."[22]

The muddy mess probably affected the engineers more than the other doughboys. There is no question that everyone was wet and miserable, but the engineers were the ones responsible for maintaining the trenches, roads, and dugouts that were inundated with water and mud. One of the division's infantrymen recalled that the engineers "labored incessantly" to keep the roads in the best shape possible. Additional groups of engineers worked with the artillery, tanks, signal corps, and the in-

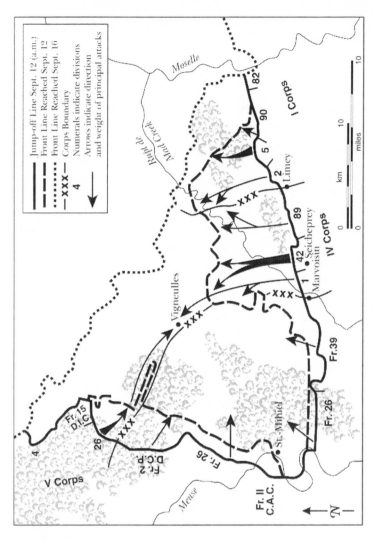

5. American First Army plan of attack at Saint-Mihiel on September 12, 1918. *Source:* American Battle Monuments Commission, *American Armies and Battlefields in Europe,* 109.

fantry.[23] Several companies of the 117th Engineers were divided between the division's two infantry brigades—the 83rd and 84th Brigades—and participated directly in the attack. These engineers were responsible for marking jump-off and sector boundaries, removing enemy wire with cutters and bangalore torpedoes, searching for and destroying German traps, and preparing routes for the advance of tanks, infantry, and artillery.[24]

In the 117th Engineers, Companies A, B, D, and E assigned one platoon of wire cutters to cut paths through their own barbed wire and guide the infantry to their attack positions. Another platoon from each company assisted the tanks, and two platoons accompanied the artillery.[25] The engineers marked positions for the infantry units at the front and paths for those forces to follow once the attack began.[26] Father Duffy explained, "It is a miracle of fate or of organization that the units were able to find their positions on such a night, but they all got where they belonged and found the lines neatly taped by Colonel Johnson's [commander of the 117th Engineers] excellent body of engineers."[27]

A sense of nervous anticipation swept through the lines as the doughboys moved to their jump-off positions the night of September 11–12. For the first time in the war, an American force of approximately two hundred thousand men was going to carry out a major offensive. "Oh, boy!," wrote one sergeant, "We are close to the front. A thrill comes to everyone approaching the great adventure again."[28] The night was strangely quiet until 1:00 a.m. on September 12, when seemingly all at once the night sky exploded with the largest Allied artillery bombardment of the war. The allies used three thousand guns of varying calibers to fire 1.1 million artillery rounds against the German positions between 1:00 and 5:00 a.m.[29] The bombardment "hammered the Boche lines and batteries," wrote one second lieutenant. "It seemed as if all the artillery in France had suddenly opened up. . . . The sky was red with big flashes . . . and the explosions of the heavier shells made the ground tremble."[30] Another soldier recorded in his diary, "At about 1 a.m. one of the most terrible barrages I have yet witnessed begins. The noise is deafening. The sky as light as day, words of mine can never describe the scene."[31] The artillery fire, mixed with the almost constant rain, tormented the soldiers. At approximately 4:40 a.m., twenty minutes before the men went over the top, the barrage intensified, falling "like a tornado of hot hail and lightning upon the enemy front lines. . . . The very heavens seemed [to] be on fire, the light of the bursting shells and the roar of the countless guns produced an unearthly uproar and tumult of noise so great that men had to shout into each other's ears in order to be heard and understood."[32]

The men in the trenches carried only the minimum of equipment—reserve rations, ammunition, and one blanket apiece—as they prepared to go over the top. They left everything else behind to be picked up later. The day before the attack the men received 250 rounds of ammunition and some grenades.[33] While excited, most of the troops felt miserable. One corporal explained, "We arose to our feet, leaning against the muddy banks. Our hands were slimy with the oozy clay. Our feet now felt the chill of penetrating cold."[34] A captain reported that "the trenches were literally jammed with men, nerves on edge and straining at the leash."[35] At 5:00 a.m. the officers blew their whistles signaling the men to go over the top.

The men crossed into no-man's-land with some of the best support provided during the war for an attacking force. Almost fifteen hundred allied airplanes provided support in the daytime, and more than eighty tanks, commanded by Col. George S. Patton, moved forward with the infantry.[36] While the tanks proved of little value, the air support served the infantry well.

Waves of American doughboys climbed out of the trenches at the sound of their officers' whistles. One lieutenant, who was leading a platoon, described how he and his men "moved forward under a rolling barrage of artillery and machine guns, a smoke screen covered our front and it was a very queer sensation to be moving forward through the smoke not knowing whether the whistling of bullets over our heads was coming from the enemy or from our own units in our rear, we had the feeling we might walk into this damable machine gun fire most any minute."[37] Another officer, observing the attack from a distance, described no-man's-land as "dotted with thousands of soldiers, like busy brown ants crawling over burnt sugar."[38]

In most cases, engineers preceded the advancing infantry. "In front of every platoon," one doughboy recalled, "were the California and South Carolina engineers with wire cutters and bangalore torpedoes to cut or to blow out any wire entanglements that remained in the path of the infantry."[39] A reporter for the *Boston Globe* described what the engineers and infantry had to cut through: "Nowhere else in our experience did we see so much wire as there was in this sector. Elsewhere there had been belts, anywhere up to 30 yards across; here belt followed belt, and there were literally miles of wire entanglements."[40] Fortunately for the engineers and infantry, much of the wire was old and rusted, and the Germans put up less resistance than anticipated.

The timing of the attack caught the Germans by surprise. In June they had made the decision to withdraw from the salient and planned to gradually leave the area over an eight-day period because they believed their position was too vulnerable to a pincer attack like the one the Americans eventually launched. Gen. Max von Gallowitz, the commander of the German troops in the salient, ordered the withdrawal to begin on the night of September 11 not knowing the immediacy of the American offensive. The timing of the German withdrawal could not have been more advantageous for the American forces, as they caught the German forces on the move from one prepared defensive position to another. Instead of defending from established positions, the Germans were forced to fight on the run—a very difficult proposition.[41] "It certainly was not like the fighting on the Ourcq," one officer recalled. "The morale of the Germans seemed to have sunk to almost nothing, and once the main [defense] system was penetrated they offered little resistance."[42]

The American offensive was a major success from a military standpoint, as the infantry achieved its first day's objectives by noon on September 12.[43] The army's official assessment of the battle's first day claimed, "The troops passed through the enemy's barrage without severe casualties and overcame the resistance of the enemy machine gunners in the forward positions."[44] Furthermore, within forty-eight hours of the start of the offensive, the salient had been eliminated and the American forces had captured more than sixteen thousand German prisoners and 440 artillery pieces.[45]

The Germans were impressed by the bravery of the American soldiers. An assessment made after the interrogation of German prisoners found that "they regard Americans as fresh and vigorous fighters of high courage and stamina. The Americans now, they say, are like the Germans in 1914."[46] There was evidently some confusion within the German ranks as to which American units they were fighting. One lieutenant recalled that "one of the German prisoners, who met us here and at Chateau Thierry [the Battle of the Ourcq], but did not realize we were at both places, said that America only had two good divisions—the 42nd and the Rainbow."[47] Although the Germans may have been mixed up and did not realize that the 42nd and the Rainbow were one in the same, they did recognize the division as a first-rate fighting unit.

The official report's matter-of-fact description of the resistance belied the bravery of the American soldiers and the physical costs of the attack. While the total casualties proved relatively light compared to the battle of the Ourcq River and later the battle of the Meuse-Argonne, they were still horrendous for those involved. One lieutenant described how one German shell "landed in the middle of my platoon and hit a man from the engineers on the thigh, practically taking his leg off and tearing him up pretty badly. He died in a short time."[48] Another corporal later wrote,

A large shell had made a direct hit upon four boys. All were dead. Limbs were mangled, bodies were torn. It was a sight revolting beyond description. Of one of my comrades I could find only small fragments of his poor body. None were larger than my hand . . . with the exception . . . there lay his head, jerked completely from his body. . . . The powder-blackened face of a young Jewish boy stared immobile into eternity. Nearby was his hand which had been popped off at the arm just back of the wrist. . . . And I looked back at the others. . . . Their spent distorted bodies with muscles still twitching.[49]

Another private, who was part of the medical detachment of a division advancing near the 42nd, pondered, "Can I ever forget the sight? Shells going in all directions and the rat-tat-tat of the machine guns." He then went on to describe the wounded he treated and the dead he found. The last soldier he found dead that day was a corporal who "is completely riddled with machine gun bullets & both leg bones sticking up through his clothing where he has fallen."[50] By the end of the battle, the Rainbow

Division had suffered more than twelve hundred casualties, including nine engineers killed in action and another eighteen wounded.[51]

SEPTEMBER 26, 1918

Dearest Marty,

. . . You see we have settled down at last and are holding a sector of the line just as respectable soldiers should. Ever since the first of June until now we have been traveling around looking for drives and when we couldn't find one, why we made one. Doing a weeks work here and there or hiking or drilling or riding box-cars. It's an exciting life with new scenes all the time and I like most of it. One great trouble is that I never write while we're traveling. When we hike we have to work too hard and we usually throw away all our paper anyway. And when we ride trains there's usually a long hike at end of the trip.

But at last we're back at work on a sector once more. We get tasks to do—work hard and finish early. Yesterday I started working days and we finished our days' work before noon—Again today. There's absolutely nothing to do but write & I want to write to someone so why not?

We thought we were in the war again last night but nothing has developed in our sector. However I think the Boches are being taught a lesson on our left. A bombardment started here at about midnight, both sides contributing and lasted till 8 this morning. It's still going on at 5 this afternoon on the left, more or less heavy all the time. I can't say I enjoyed it much last night in my little tar paper shack, but no shells came very near so finally I slept in all the noise. They usually shoot at the [artillery] batteries, but I have seen their aim pretty poor. Then they might shell the whole woods. In that case I should probably have slept in an open field somewhere.

This a.m. we went out to work as usual tho they were still shelling some in our path. One time we stopped on a little hill to wait for them to stop throwing shells in the valley ahead. They quit soon and we went on thru. They must have been using gas there as all of us got more or less of it. However it was only sneezing gas and therefore harmless. Just affects the eyes and makes one sneeze and cough. [52] They send that over because soldiers don't notice it then right afterward send the poison gas. Of course everyone puts on his mask but one can't keep it on and cough or sneeze. These Boches have lovely traps for one don't they? But I guess we usually give them about as good as they send and sometimes I think go them one better. . . . Goodbye Marty and love from the one who does not forget you.

Brownie

Brownie and the remainder of the 42nd Division maintained positions around Saint-Mihiel after the battle. It was a time for rest, resupply, and recuperation. The engineers constructed a new trench system, while the remainder of the division rested, trained, and prepared for future operations. The men's focus briefly left the difficulties of the battlefield and returned to the inconvenience of the environment, in particular the lice. [53]

While the Rainbow rested, the largest American operation of the war began in the Meuse-Argonne region of France. The period of late September and early October proved a pivotal time as the collapse of the Central powers accelerated. The offensive began on September 26 and lasted until the end of the war. The 42nd Division was unable to participate in the opening stages of the offensive because of its involvement at Saint-Mihiel. However, the artillery barrage Brownie described on the night of September 25–26 was an effort made by the AEF to divert German attention from the opening of the Meuse-Argonne offensive. The 42nd remained around Saint-Mihiel until the end of September when it began its move to the Meuse-Argonne. [54]

AUGUST 15, 1918

Dearest Marty,

It seems ages since I wrote you, but in reality, it's only about a week. Perhaps what makes it seem so long is because I've had so many letters from you lately. . . . Many, many thanks Marty. . . .

This is one day later, Marty. I was too lazy to finish last night. The boys have come back from Paris and I've been entertained by their yarns. No more passes are to be issued at present evidently and I'm much disappointed. . . . But still there's time yet and I'm going to visit the city if I can. You know who I'd like to have for company—Guess who. Wouldn't that be enjoyable if it could be so. But we can't have everything we want. Even the Kaiser can't go to Paris now.

I owe you so many letters I never will be able to answer them all. During the past week I must have received ten from you. . . .

Now honest Marty, you should have had letters from me of both July 4th & 6th and then at least one more before the 14th. After that I don't know because my experience in war commenced then. During a terrible bombardment the 14th a lot of letters were lost and scattered thru the field but didn't think that there was but one letter to you among them.[55] I must stop writing now Marty but here's a good-night and love.

I hope you won't think it strange to have me write in ink again. I borrowed this pen, as well as the paper. We sure are out of luck for almost everything up here. I don't know how I am going to mail this letter as there are no enveloppes that I know of in the Company. . . .

We've had some lovely days lately and I passed one or two lovely moonlight nights out at the front working. Remember some moonlight nights passed not working. Sometimes I despise this war and our separation Marty. Do you? Still I know that what must be will be. If you can wait my Marty I know I can cause that's all I've been doing for more than a year now. . . . I'm glad I'm here anyway for I wouldn't be satisfied or you couldn't be satisfied with me were I in the States now. We've had our good times in the past & I'll always look forward to many more in the future and so wait for the end of all this tiresome war. . . . Goodbye Marty and love from the one who does not forget you.

Brownie

Brownie's efforts to keep writing Marty obviously proved a sore spot in their relationship. He felt compelled in his September 21 letter to explain that he had actually written some letters that had been lost in one of the German artillery barrages. Marty continued to write, however, and their relationship did not suffer much. Their letters clearly indicate the difficulties of maintaining wartime relationships. Brownie was often too busy to write and/or faced shortages of paper and writing utensils, and he was not the only one. A Rainbow officer implored his mother in early October to understand the infrequency of his letters: "Paper is not to be had in a situation like this."[56] The soldiers' constant movement and participation in battles played havoc on the mail service and resupply efforts. Brownie's only recourse was to constantly reassure Marty of his love and to remind her that the war would not last forever.

Although the United States had been in the war for only a relatively short time, Brownie and the 42nd Division had more actual experience than almost any other American unit. The division's effectiveness on the battlefield won the accolades of its enemies and allies alike and guaranteed its involvement in any significant American operation. While it could not lead off the attack in the Meuse-Argonne because of its participation in the battle of Saint-Mihiel, there was little question that it would join the attack in the near future. Brownie and the other Rainbow veterans faced the coming battle with trepidation. They were no longer naïve about war's realities.

SIX

The Meuse-Argonne Offensive
and the End of the War

The largest American offensive of World War I began on September 26 when the AEF attacked German forces in the Argonne Forest between the Meuse and Aisne rivers, approximately twenty miles north of Verdun. Nine divisions of U.S. troops, totaling more than 200,000 men, struck German positions in the densely wooded forest with the goal of cutting the Carignan-Sedan-Mezieres Railroad. Six weeks later the battle was over and the United States had suffered more than 120,000 casualties while advancing thirty-four miles.[1] The 42nd Division was near Saint-Mihiel at the start of the offensive and only moved into the Meuse-Argonne region in early October when it received orders to act as infantry reserves. Its climatic involvement came on October 14 when it launched an attack against the center of the German lines. The Germans provided stiff resistance until near the end, but the American forces and their allies on other areas of the front eventually prevailed, and Germany surrendered on November 11.

World War I reached its climax between late September and early November 1918. American forces began the Meuse-Argonne offensive on September 26 as one part of a larger Allied operation along the western front.[2] The American objective was to drive German forces out of this sector. General Pershing commanded the rapidly growing American First Army of more than one million men and hoped to advance through approximately ten miles of German defenses in a few days. Much to his chagrin, the German forces proved stout defenders and the American soldiers too inexperienced. Only after extremely protracted fighting and high casualties did the U.S. forces ultimately triumph.

The Meuse-Argonne offensive offered Pershing the opportunity to prove the capabilities of the AEF. While the American First Army had been successful in its initial battle at Saint-Mihiel in mid-September, America's allies were still not convinced that U.S. officers and soldiers were ready to wage a major operation on their own. The Americans could not have picked a worse place to test their mettle, since the Meuse-Argonne region contained significant natural defensive positions that the Germans exploited fully to create almost impenetrable lines. The Meuse River to the east was unfordable and the hills on its east bank gave the Germans a clear view of the battlefield and excellent defensive positions and artillery sites. The Argonne Forest to the west was a formidable barrier. The Montfaucon Hills, with a height of almost eleven hundred feet, dominated the center.[3] The terrain made the battlefield even more imposing. "Thick woods, tangled underbrush, scarred trees, gaping shell holes, deep ravines, and lofty ridges," wrote one of the Rainbow division's lieutenants, "united to make a country already desolate and difficult still more forbidding."[4] A private in the Seventy-eighth Division described the region as "a cross between a volcanic eruption and a section of hell set aside to cool."[5]

The Germans maximized the natural advantages by building a series of defensive positions along what the Allies called the Hindenburg Line: Giselher Stellung, Kriemhilde Stellung, and Streya Stellung.[6] Each position was heavily defended with barbed wire, machine gun nests, and trenches. Furthermore, the Germans had carefully mapped the entire sector for their artillery and mortars to use. Pershing later claimed, "The net result of the four years' struggle on this ground was a German defensive system of unusual depth and strength and a wide zone of utter devastation, itself a serious obstacle to offensive operations."[7] The American soldiers, in other words, were walking into a death trap.

The difficulties faced by the AEF were even greater than just the German defenses. American forces faced a logistical nightmare because Pershing had insisted that the AEF could carry out an assault against Saint-Mihiel starting September 12 and still be ready to attack in the Meuse-Argonne sector at the end of the month. Further, he and his staff believed that the battle of Saint-Mihiel had to be a success; therefore, they placed the best-trained and most experienced American divisions at the vanguard of that assault. Although successful, these divisions were not available for use at the beginning of the Meuse-Argonne offensive. In the initial assaults, Pershing had to rely instead on divisions that had little or no experience and were not fully trained.[8] One sergeant in the 42nd later recalled the poor training of some of his men as they made preparations for the battle:

> While giving a short talk on the necessity of strict obedience, I was floored by one of the boys, who spoke for his four or five companies, that, although they were anxious and eager to do exactly what I said, if they didn't, it would be because they didn't understand, as their service and training was of the most meager. They had fired a service rifle about ten times, that is, about ten rounds. They had never fired a live hand grenade, one of the best weapons of the infantry in a tight corner. They didn't know what a rifle grenade looked like, and, to make it complete, had never had bayonet instruction.[9]

An additional complication presented by the battle of Saint-Mihiel was that the AEF had to transfer more than 600,000 troops, 900,000 tons of supplies, almost 4,000 artillery pieces, and 90,000 horses sixty miles from that battle to the Meuse-Argonne region. This had to be accomplished using three poorly maintained roads in rainy weather and in a week's time.[10] One lieutenant claimed that "the roads were very bad, having been blown up in many places by the Boche in his retirement, and even where they have not been blown up or blocked by felling trees across them, they are muddy and deeply cut up by the heavy continuous traffic."[11]

The offensive can be broken into three broad phases: the initial attack on September 26, a second advance beginning on October 4, and the final thrust starting on October 14, which culminated in the final collapse of German positions in early November. Nine generally inexperienced divisions—the 4th, 28th, 33rd, 35th, 37th, 77th, 79th, 80th, and 91st—spearheaded the initial attack along a twenty-one-mile-long front and progressed slowly.[12] They faced strong opposition, formidable terrain, and dreary weather. The smoke from the artillery fire and the fog caused great confusion. This combination was too much for some of the men and limited the pace and effectiveness of the advance.

As the first wave of doughboys left the jump-off point, they encountered thick concentrations of barbed wire, in some places more than eight feet wide and three feet high.[13] A soldier remembered how the first wave was advancing through the wire "when, from every direction, German machine-gun fire assaulted them. Many of them crumbled at once. The second wave—which included me—lay waiting to follow them, horrified by their dying screams. . . . The next few minutes were among the worst of the war for me as we lay helpless to aid, listening to our friends being torn to pieces by gunfire."[14] Another doughboy vividly recalled the devastation of the first day: "I walked by one man. . . . He had one eye . . . hanging out of his cheek by a thick white string. Gave me a hell of a start. . . . The poor devil was still alive."[15] Later the same day the same soldier stepped on what he "thought was a dust-covered sack of grain but when it gave way and oozed maroon-colored mud at several points," he knew otherwise. He wrote in horror, "[It] must have been a quadruple or quintuple amputee."[16] By the end of the first day the First American Army had made little progress and was in bad shape.[17]

The next several days did not get any better. A lieutenant colonel, who was dazed by a nearby explosion, remembered the first thing he "saw was a severed foot, it had been cut off just above the ankle as though with a giant cleaver. The foot was sitting upright in its army shoe, and the bloody stump was a sickening sight." After initially thinking it was his own foot, he realized it belonged to one of his comrades.[18] Those who survived their initial wounding, like this lieutenant colonel, faced the awful effort of getting to an aid station. There were not enough stretcher-bearers to carry all of the wounded, and even when a soldier reached an aid station he was not assured of immediate care. A corporal came across one aid station with hundreds of wounded soldiers and saw that "many had their arms and legs hanging on by threads, others were shot in the chest, head and other parts of the body. It was such a piteous and sorrowful sight."[19]

By the end of September the fighting had decimated many of the divisions that led the attack and had left them in dire need of relief. Eight divisions, including several of the more experienced ones from the battle of Saint-Mihiel, renewed the general attack on October 4 with the goal of breaking through the Kriemhilde Stellung. The results were very much the same, as the Americans advanced only a little ways at tremendous cost. The third advance, beginning on October 14, saw the American forces, including the Rainbow Division, break through some of the German defenses. However, it was not until early November that the AEF achieved the objectives it had set for the first week of the battle.

The 42nd Division was more than sixty miles from the Argonne Forest when the battle began. Its only involvement in the opening stages of the offensive was to launch diversionary artillery barrages and infantry raids near Saint-Mihiel in hopes of confusing the Germans as to the location of the main attack. The division received its orders on September 29 to prepare to embark and on October 1 began to move to the region of the American offensive.[20] The move was difficult. One sergeant wrote, "Our engineers are busy building bridges across this forsaken country, for shell holes are so thick that a gun or even a cart can't start across it without upsetting. In fact, it is all a foot soldier can do to walk across it."[21] As the division traveled to the Argonne, it "marched into a dark and dank Fôret d'Apremont, where on either side of the road were the unburied dead of battles years before. The whitened skeletons shrouded with rotten rags of French horizon blue could be seen all through the grass and newly sprouted trees."[22] Once the division arrived, and for almost half of October, it served as reserve infantry of the First American Army.[23]

On October 12 the division moved to the front lines.[24] This move was a particularly sobering experience for the men because evidence of the previous weeks of fighting were everywhere. One doughboy recalled, "Our route lay through the most devastated area I have ever seen, forests and towns reduced to splinters and rubble, and mud, deep mud, everywhere. . . . Any semblance to a woods had totally disappeared. It was a sea of mud and stumps with foxholes everywhere."[25] A colonel in the 42nd Division wrote in his diary, "The desolation of the battlefield is beyond description. Many dead Americans and Germans everywhere. Dead horses along every road. Every building and tree destroyed and the ground one mass of muddy shell holes."[26] Another private offered a particularly poignant view of the battlefield: "You had to do some fancy footwork to avoid stepping on the dead that covered the ground. I had never before seen so many bodies. There must have been a thousand American and German dead in the valley between the two ridges. They were an awful sight, in all the grotesque positions of men killed by violence." He then added, "Once I looked down and was terribly shocked. There was a young German soldier with red hair and freckles, eyes staring at the sky—and he looked just like me."[27]

While the 42nd waited for the order to attack on October 12 and 13, its soldiers prepared for the upcoming attack, enduring miserable weather. The doughboys lived in their trenches and foxholes, only venturing out on occasional patrols. The only constants were the drumbeat of the artillery fire, the rain, and the cold. [28] The night preceding the attack was particularly dreary. One lieutenant recalled, "October 14th dawned dark, misty, and forbidding. It had rained all night, and the men, still wearing summer underclothing, with but one blanket apiece and no overcoats, rose stiffly from their beds in the mud."[29]

Pershing ordered the 42nd and several other divisions to renew the American offensive on October 14 against the strongest positions in the German lines—the Kriemhilde Stellung. The 42nd Division's chaplain wrote, "It was a well prepared and strongly wired position consisting of three lines of wires and trenches. The first rows of wire were breast high and as much as twenty feet wide, all bound together in small squares by iron supports so that it was almost impossible for artillery to destroy it unless the whole ground was beaten flat."[30] Behind the main line were several weaker, yet still formidable defensive positions. Henry Reilly, who was in the Argonne with the 42nd Division, remembered the deadly environment:

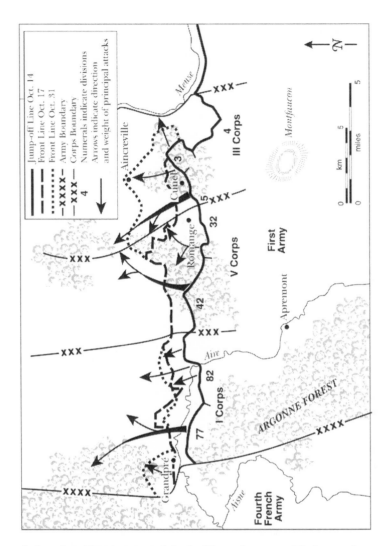

6. American First Army attack in the Meuse-Argonne with the 42nd Division in the center, October 14, 1918. *Source: United States Army in the World War*, vol. 9, 270.

The situation which now confronted the Rainbow was very different [from the Aisne-Marne front]. The Germans occupied an entrenched and well wired natural position running along ridges and the crests of hills. The Rainbow was in the open on ground everywhere dominated by the German position. On some large sectors the German positions flanked the ground the Rainbow was to advance over. At points giving a wide field of fire to the front, the Germans had concrete machine gun pill boxes in the front bands of their barbed wire."[31]

The October 14 attack "marked the beginning of three days of the fiercest fighting experienced by the whole division in the whole war."[32] The attack began with a powerful artillery barrage at 3:30 a.m. and was followed by an infantry advance along a three-and-half-mile-long front two hours later.[33] The AEF's official assessment of the October 14 attack noted, "All advances of our troops were met by violent machine-gun activity."[34] The division's summary of intelligence for the day claimed the Germans used airplanes, artillery, machine guns, and infantry to resist the American advance. The German aircraft were particularly bothersome because they controlled the skies.[35] "We were up against a tough proposition," one lieutenant wrote, "with the Huns fighting like madmen and only giving in when absolutely forced to do so."[36]

The main target on October 14 was Hill 288, and it fell only after its garrison was surrounded and virtually annihilated.[37] The individual doughboy accounts are gripping. "Just imagine walking behind a line of bursting shells—our barrage and being *in* a line of bursting shells—German. And add to that the fire of machine guns. Bullets cut the grass at our feet, sailed over us, and some of them stopped, having done their little deeds."[38] "I have vivid memories," one soldier later wrote, "of . . . Corporal Enters and Private 'Red' Hern . . . taking a few steps forward after having been decapitated by German artillery fire."[39] Another doughboy remembered the effects of a direct hit by a German artillery shell on a neighboring foxhole: "At dawn, we looked around and soon came across what appeared to be a piece of roast beef strapped by a web belt, and the initials 'ws' were burned in the belt. Those were the mortal remains of Bill Sheahan."[40]

The incredibly bloody fighting continued for three more days before Pershing ordered an end to the attack and consolidation of the newly won territory. When the doughboys attacked again on the afternoon of October 14 and the next morning, they "faced powerful obstacles of terrain, organization, and enemy resistance" and had to overcome strong barbed wire defenses "under the frontal and enfilading fire of enemy machine guns and artillery." Throughout the fighting, the enemy resisted furiously and showed no willingness to withdraw or to surrender. [41]

The main objective on October 15 was La Tuilerie Farm, and the Germans took advantage of the heavily wooded and sloped terrain as well as strong layers of barbed wire to resist the American attacks. German soldiers "offered grim battle" and were only driven back after two days of "prolonged and bitter fighting." [42] October 16 marked the climax of this phase of the battle of Meuse-Argonne, as a brigade of the 42nd succeeded in penetrating the Kriemhilde Stellung near the Côte de Châtillon and overcoming most German resistance. [43]

The Rainbow Division's engineers, including Brownie, played a prominent role in the fighting from October 14 to 17. They served as the division's infantry reserve while also fulfilling their usual roles as engineers. Companies C and F of the 117th Engineers performed functions similar to those at Saint-Mihiel and actually preceded the infantry in the attack, cutting paths through the layers of barbed wire and other obstacles. [44] They had a very difficult task since the Germans anticipated the attack and had well-prepared defenses. After the battle, the engineers' "bodies littered the ground and corpses were hanging on the wire." [45] One infantryman, observing the 117th's activities, remarked, "Some of our regular engineers tried to cut a passage through the wire, covered by riflemen and several of our machine guns. But the Germans were firing from concealed pill boxes behind the first belt of wires. . . . Their machine gun fire killed or wounded all those engineers." [46] Despite the losses, the engineers did manage to overcome the German defensive obstacles and clear paths for the advancing infantry.

Other than the companies that went over the top with the infantry, most of the engineers filled in shell holes, repaired and built roads, and buried the dead. [47] They had to maintain old roads and build new ones to permit the resupply of the advancing units. These tasks became even more difficult as the infantry advanced because the newly conquered territory consisted of countless shell holes. The burying of the dead was also extremely difficult. Not only did the engineers have to bury some of their comrades from their own division, but they also had to bury the bodies of American and German soldiers who had been fighting in that area since the beginning of the battle.

By the end of October 16 the attack had run its course, and the AEF entered a two-week period of consolidating positions, rest, recovery, and retraining. The AEF had suffered at all levels, and it needed this time "to reorganize and complete arrangements for a powerful blow."[48] The Germans maintained a defensive stance but strongly resisted any American incursion toward their lines. As daily intelligence reports from the 42nd described, "The enemy infantry [is] in force and with its machine gun nests offers an unyielding front to the movements of our patrols. [Rifle] Fire is immediate and sharp at the approach of our men and the enemy uses his fire as a machine gun aiming point . . . and through which he pours a devastating fire when threatened with attack."[49] A later report added, "Any visible movement in our lines is immediately fired upon by enemy snipers with rifles and machine guns."[50] This defensive approach continued through the month, with artillery fire added to the deadly machine guns.[51]

Although the Germans remained on the defensive and the AEF limited its offensive activity to patrols, many American veterans remembered the last two weeks of October as some of the most difficult of the war. Every division was short of men. For example, the Rainbow Division needed an additional seventy-six hundred men in late October to fill its ranks.[52] The remaining men were exhausted, and "the lice and the dirt had so lowered their vitality that they succumbed to even minor ailments."[53] An exhausted lieutenant opined, "there is only mud, more mud, and almost unbroken artillery fire—and cooties. I don't know which bothers me the most, the noise of heavy guns day and night, or the tireless efforts of the cooties—also day and night!"[54] Another doughboy explained how "his shirt appeared to be literally crawling, undulating, rippling with movement."[55]

The lice were not the limit of the suffering. The weather was generally rainy and cold. One private wrote in his diary on October 20, "We were *completely* water soaked. It has rained all night, so cold I can hardly move."[56] The Rainbow's Father Duffy later wrote that the last two weeks of October "were the dreariest, draggiest days we spent in the war. The men lay out on the bare hillsides in little pits they had dug for themselves, the bottoms of which were turned into mud by frequent rains. They had one blanket apiece, and were without overcoats, underwear, or socks, in the unpleasant climate of a French Autumn. They were dirty, lousy, thirsty; often hungry; and nearly every last man was sick."[57]

The daily artillery barrages and intermittent machine gun fire only added to the misery. "We were facing," remembered one Rainbow veteran,

> what proved to be for us the cruelest days of the war. For weeks now we had been under almost constant shell-fire, snatching what little sleep we could in miserable foxholes, always wet, always cold. Life depended on a matter of feet and inches—whether the next shell would fall a few feet or yards away or whether it would find its mark. We had seen our men change before our eyes, their faces becoming gaunt and gray, their lips thin and blue, their nerves ragged from lack of sleep; their clothes, their hair, their stubble of beard matted with the slimy mud of the foxholes.[58]

The German artillery and machine gun fire also continued to inflict casualties during this period of reorganization. A private recalled carrying a recent draftee who had been killed by a long shard of steel from a German artillery shell that "tookoff everything above his eyebrows." He added, "seeing that slick, pink brain-pan on top of his truncated head didn't do any of us any good."[59] Another doughboy, who saw German machine gun fire kill a friend right next to him in late October, wrote, "I can never forget the death gurgle in his throat."[60] The shell fire did not discriminate against animals. A doughboy wrote home describing how "a shell came over and hit a tree, not 50 feet away, tearing down the tree and killing one officer and his horse, two mules, and tore off the leg of another horse nearby. It took a doughboy five shots to kill the horse that had its leg blown off."[61]

It was during these last two weeks of October that Brownie was gassed, although exactly when is unclear.[62] The Germans launched thousands of gas shells during this time, including a large gas attack on the night of October 27 that "was heavier and extended over more terrain than has happened for some days." They attacked different parts of the 42nd Division's sector at different times during the night with sneezing and phosgene gas. All together the Germans fired 4,200 artillery rounds, including 2,000 gas shells.[63] One soldier remembered that on October 27 "the gas was so thick you could cut it with a knife."[64] A doctor with the Rainbow claimed the gas casualties were "numerous and severe."[65] Effects of the gas depended on the type encountered, but most attacked the respiratory system. A corporal in the 117th, who was gassed earlier in the war, exclaimed, "Boy that is some feeling when you get that stuff in your system. The first whiff tastes and smells good, but just wait a few seconds and the nausea is awful. When that is over your chest, throat and eyes worry you."[66] Approximately 19,000 Americans were gassed in the Meuse-Argonne offensive, including 730 men from the Rainbow Division.[67]

OCTOBER 30, 1918

Dearest Marty,

I don't know whether to write excuses or not but perhaps it would be better to give some reasons for my long silence. For one we've been on the worse front we've seen so far and that's saying something.[68] Then of course nothing to write on when we were in any state of mind so that we felt like writing. And for the same reason I havn't written during the past week while wandering around Base 70. I'm feeling better in fact never was too sick to write but I positively couldn't get any stationary. One would expect to find at least that here but it was lacking. This I'm using has just been issued.

It sure has been a wonderful treat for me in the hospital here. Just the bath and the bed alone are something too good to be true. After months of dog-tents, the last one muddy, rainy and cold. Also, and not the least I'm rid of the cooties for the first time since July. It's going to be hard to get used to the old way again, but already I've begun to miss the old bunch—wondering how they are making out, or if they are still on the front. I hope not, because it was too tough to stay long. Lots has happened since

I wrote—naturally it has been so long. Lots of letters and several from you. Also two *Cosmos* and I read them thru. Really just to look at those magazines with their nice pictures and good stories and nice paper even to the ads are enough to make one homesick. One kind of homesickness—the kind we like. Thanks.

We've been having wonderful weather for four days now. Just like Indian Summer but perhaps that's because we are rather far South. . . .

Marty, I'm just longing always more and more to get back to see you, and the news lately has looked encouraging. I hope they aren't just kidding us along. I must stop now Marty but I'll send you lots of love and more.

NOVEMBER 9, 1918

I imagine this is the chance of my life so I'm going to write you a letter. I mean the best chance I've ever had in France to write one. Now I'm in an Eng. Replacement Camp in one of the large cities of Western France. So you see I'm nearer you than I've been in over a year. Not much nearer tho after—unless Germany signs the armistice. I wonder will she? If she does the whole world is going to be happy and if not—well then I suppose I must have some more chances to try to make them wish they had.

It seems a long time now since I left the front. I suppose it's just as muddy and rainy and miserable as ever but after all I somehow wish I were up there again. Guess I miss the boys in the outfit or perhaps it's because I don't want to miss any of the Rainbow doings. But I ought to reach them during the coming week, so why worry.

It sure is funny the way they do things in the army. I'm no longer in the 117th. After one has been away ten days his record goes to a Central Record Office and is kept there till the soldier goes back, if he does. Of course he does go back if he's in Class A. At first he belongs to some certain hospital and when he leaves there he becomes what they term "A Casual." That's what I am now and it sure is a casual sort of existance. First I spent about three days right near the hospital in what they call a Convalescent Camp. Then we got on a train and rode all night. We landed in a place they call a "Rest Camp." I stayed there all day and that night was sent out to this place. It took two nights and days to get here and we passed thru the very place I had just left. And all the while getting away from the outfit, so imagine the trip to go back. Two nights I slept on the train and last night in some sort of Red Cross Hut near the station. Surely it's a Casual life. You always are taken care of but you may get there or you may not. But you always get somewhere and there's always something for you to eat, and someone to look out for you. For instance if you get off at some large place to look around there's no danger of being lost because there are M.P.s there to see that you don't leave the station. So here I am at the receiving station of the Eng. Replacement Camp awaiting reclassification. I think that's what it is. Now I'm in Class A so probably I'll continue in that Class. If I do I'll soon be back with the boys on the front and perhaps in Germany. Things are coming our way now.

This army is sure a huge and complicated machine. This of course is the first time I've ever seen this end of it.

I don't know what you'll be thinking of me Marty after all these long silences of mine. Really I love to write to you and if I had half a chance I'd prove it. Tonight is the first time in months that I have had all the stationary I wanted. I know it's hard for you to write me when you never receive any letters. It's a month since I heard from you so I can appreciate how it is. I know that your letters are at the Company, tho. Must quit Marty but if I stay here I'll make up some of the lost time.

Au revoir Marty
Love from
Brownie

Replenished and resupplied, the AEF renewed its offensive against the Germans on November 1 with the 42nd Division in reserve. Unlike during the first five weeks of the offensive, the German resistance was relatively light and the AEF, as a whole, had much more success than previously. The 42nd moved back to the front on November 5 and remained there five days. The division's official summary of intelligence from November 6 reported that the soldiers faced harassing machine gun fire of little consequence as they advanced. The relative lack of resistance reflected not only the decline in German fighting effectiveness but also an increase in the Americans' skills. While the AEF emerged from the Meuse-Argonne offensive triumphant, it was severely bloodied. It destroyed German resistance in the sector, took more than 25,000 prisoners, inflicted close to 100,000 casualties, and captured numerous pieces of equipment over the course of the offensive. The price for the 1.2 million American soldiers who participated in the battle was terribly high, however. The AEF sustained more than 26,000 dead and 95,000 wounded, including more than 4,200 in the Rainbow Division and 90 in the 117th Engineers.[69]

NOVEMBER 12, 1918 (Angers, France)

Dearest Marty,

I must write you tonight—things have been so interesting and events have been so happy. Does it seem possible to you that the war is over? I can't make it seem so someway—can I be going to the States soon? If I were on the front now it would be more real but here things are just the same only everyone is happy and celebrating. And there's no doubt that this is the end but when will we start home? More questions. It seems to me that I've read somewhere that the Divisions over here will go back as nearly as possible in the same order they came over. In that case I'd sure be lucky, and for the same reason I'm afraid now that they may try to transfer me. I have no notion that they will at that, but I'm all the anxious to see the Company I left home with. All that we think of now is "home." It's going to be hard on any of the boys that have to stay a long while after peace is declared.

There was great rejoicing all over France yesterday and last night. I got a pass and saw some of it here. This is quite a city the largest I've visited in France about 150,000 and everyone sure went wild last night. The crowds made the streets impassible, and such singing and shouting. There were thousands of French and American soldiers and they naturally were prominent in all kinds of deviltry. I had to go back to camp at 9:30 but I enjoyed it till then. There must have been some great times over there, too. Anyway we'll have them over again when we all get home. More about "I" now. That's all I write of isn't it, Marty?

To-day I was transferred to the last camp. From here men go to their organizations. . . . I've been clear across France to about fifteen different camps and barracks and from here I go right back. Very long trips and the trains are far from fast. I'm hoping our outfit won't be one of those to occupy a point in Germany.

I must quit now Marty but home soon I hope & I know you hope.   Always your,

Brownie

Brownie saw the end of the war on November 11 from a temporary base for soldiers who had recovered from wounds and were ready to be returned to their previous units. There was tremendous excitement throughout Europe and in the United States at the announcement of war's end. However, the excitement was tempered by the reality of the costs of the war. The United States had suffered much less than the other Allies who experienced more than three million dead, but its losses were still severe [70]: 53,402 Americans either died in battle or from their wounds; another 63,114 died from other causes, principally the Spanish flu epidemic of 1918–19; and finally, 204,200 were wounded. [71] Brownie emerged from the war relatively unscathed and, like the rest of the more than two million doughboys in Europe, was anxious to return home.

Conclusion

The war's end brought elation as well as additional challenges. The soldiers experienced hope and frustration; the AEF wrestled with occupying part of Germany, maintaining discipline, and sending troops home; and demobilization burdened the American government. Brownie continued to write Marty from November until his return home in February 1919, even though Marty's letters from the same time period did not reach him until after his arrival in the United States. Like Brownie and Marty's relationship, the United States successfully completed the transition to peacetime. Brownie and Marty were reunited in February, and Americans tried to put the war behind them.

NOVEMBER 15, 1918 (Angers, France)

Dearest Marty,

You see I havn't yet left the city so I'm still without news from you or home. This is the last step before going to the outfit but I seem to be stuck here. Not a very pleasant place to stick either because they drill us casuals all day long. A couple of fellows who came up here with me decided to miss drill the first afternoon and now they're in the "can".[1] So I decided to meet all formations.

I have been . . . in this camp for three days now and it's a nice place outside of drilling. It consists of five story barracks all of brick and reminds me of Ft. Slocum. The barracks practically enclose the parade ground which is perfectly level and must cover about six acres. It's a swell place all right—too good for war. Of course it was built in peace times the same as our good Regular Army barracks. I have no idea how many men are here but it must be around 3000. It's wonderful to see them feed the men here. Talk about feeding the animals. They run two mess lines and sometimes the lines move so fast that one has to run to keep up. They feed the bunch in about ten minutes a much shorter time than it takes to feed our little Company of 250. You sure have to move tho or they'd pour the slum down the back of your neck. . . .

Every day they post a bulletin here naming various Engr. units whose men are going out the next day. So far I've looked in vain for 117. However there are about a dozen of us here now so we ought to leave soon. I have hopes that the Rainbow may go to the U.S.A. among the first, but I hardly expect it will be toute de suite. Wouldn't that be wonderful? I can hardly imagine myself back there now.

NOVEMBER 26, 1918

The lights are rather poor in the Y this evening, but I must write just the same. Not must but I want to. I'm still at Angers—wonderful city—been in this last camp two weeks. From the looks of things I'll stay here too, till they get ready to ship me back across the pond. When that will be only the Lord and G.H.Q. [General Headquarters] know and I guess the latter hasn't decided yet.

So I've about given up hope of going back with the Rainbow Division. Of course I should like to be with them but as things now look I may beat them back so what's the difference. They sure did see all kinds of action on all the fronts and the guys who went thru it all unhurt were very lucky. Especially in the Infantry. When I enlisted all branches looked alike to me but I will admit that many [times] I've felt thankful for being in the Engineers. At one time our platoon even preceded the Infy in an advance but that was only once.[2] All this isn't very interesting now that the war is over is it Marty?

All I can think of now is going home, and until there was some talk of it I never gave it much thought. Some of the fellows are so bad that they talk of nothing else all day long. Lots are going soon and I hope to be among them. Sometimes I think I'm going soon and sometimes I think it will be three months so you see it's just suspense.

Naturally and as usual I have no mail coming. And I don't want to write to the Co. and change my address for fear of moving again soon. So I never know how you are or anything about home? It makes it rather mean but why kick? Maybe I never will get any more mail in France. But Marty the time comes for everything and uno how I look forward to seeing you again. I wonder do you ever get any mail from me.

NOVEMBER 30, 1918

I'm having a very good time doing nothing these last two days, but that only makes me remember you more. I don't think it's the doing nothing that makes me want to write but it surely gives me more time. I am still at Angers, but am at a different camp that explains why I'm resting. Of course as yesterday was Thanksgiving I should have had a holiday most anywhere, but here most every day is a holiday. . . . The first three or four days I was in Angers I passed here, and we are near the center of town. However I never go out and don't even care to go. Yesterday I should have gone out and looked around only it was such a miserable day. I've lost interest in everything in France and wouldn't give two bits to see Paris. Everything is overshadowed by the prospect of a trip home.

I havn't told you yet that I've about given up hope of going back to my outfit. You see I was ready to go back to them at just the time when they started hiking for the German frontier so naturally I couldn't be shipped till they got settled in some definite place. Then as I saw a chance to beat them back by going as a casual I decided to stay a casual. So I am supposed to be on my way home tho there's nothing very rapid about it. The joke will be on me won't it if the 42nd gets back first? And it wouldn't be a surprise to me if it did. However only time will tell.

Now my usual complaint, but no offense Marty. I would love

to hear from you and home. The last letter from you was written the 18th of September. Isn't that long, long ago? Sometimes I'm sorry I didn't go back to the 117th just to get my mail. But I'm not complaining and as I don't expect to get any more letters while in France it's not hard to do without them. It is harder to write, of course, because any letter is an inspiration for an answer.

DECEMBER 22, 1918

Do you think I have forgotten you? I havn't tho can I make you believe it? Perhaps it's because I never get any letters that I never write for surely I very seldom do write now. A while back I was expecting to go back to the States and hoped to surprise you by writing from there all at once. Perhaps I'll leave soon now, but I don't know. I'm still in Angers and won't leave before New Year's Day. Just to think that I've spent nearly two months here, since the ninth of November. . . .

Just at present I'm in Co. I, 116th. I think it's the fourth or fifth different Company to which I've been attached. We don't have to work hard luckily. My Service Record has never come and by now I don't ever expect it. . . . Already I've had too many of my friends leave me, and start back home. I've never heard from anyone in my old Co. since I left so all I know about them is that they are included in the Army of Occupation. Sometimes I wish I were up there with them. When one is with his outfit he always knows where he stands but words can't describe the standing of a casual. . . .

Now Marty I must stop. This is not much of a letter but all I know to write of. Tho, I've enjoyed myself lately and expect to have a Merry Christmas. Uno what Marty—I can't forget you and all you mean to me. It's almost exactly a year and a half ago. I'm thinking of and loving you now too-Marty.

From your own,
Brownie

Brownie was not unique in experiencing frustration in the war's aftermath. Doughboys considered their job done and only wanted to return home. The U.S. government's and the AEF's challenge was to keep the soldiers and their families as happy as possible while fulfilling obligations as an Allied power. Under the

November armistice agreement, the Allies had to control parts of Germany along the Rhine River. Unfortunately, this meant some American troops would have to perform occupation duty before going home. The United States had to maintain some forces in case of an unexpected renewal of hostilities, assign others to occupation duty on the Rhine River, and arrange the transportation of most of the soldiers home as soon as possible, all while maintaining discipline.

Brownie remained in Angers for two months as he recovered from his gassing and awaited his next orders. His initial hopes of rejoining the Rainbow Division faded as he began to focus on his return home. His stay was uneventful and actually quite pleasurable, as Angers was "claimed to be the paradise of the wounded man by everyone who passed through there."[3]

Brownie continued to write Marty almost weekly even though the last letter he received from her was written in September. The battle of the Meuse-Argonne and the disruptions of Brownie's movements prevented the delivery of her letters. It was only after he returned to the United States that he received the letters Marty wrote between late September and the end of the year, the only ones from Marty that survived the war. Besides expressing her love, Marty mainly described their families' and friends' activities. The one exception was a letter she wrote in late November. She did not know Brownie had been wounded until then.

NOVEMBER 27TH, 1918

Brownie dear—Your letter came yesterday and my mind is very much muddled—were you in the hospital because of a cold or what?[4] Why didn't you tell me? Of course I was very anxious, but I had to re-read your letter to even decide you were there. I'm awfully sorry but of course it's too late. . . .

Do I forgive you for not writing oftener? I wonder if I do? I can't decide. I'll tell you when you come home. . . .

Think of you so much & shall be so glad to see you.

Same old love
Your Marty[5]

While Brownie and Marty worried about their reunion, the

42nd Division began its administration of the area along the Rhine River. General Pershing had selected the Rainbow and four other divisions to form the American Army of Occupation because of their effectiveness on the battlefield. While other divisions were added to the occupation force, these five provided the core until the last one withdrew in August 1919. The Rainbow Division's headquarters was in Ahrweiler, and the division was responsible for supervising 122 towns in the surrounding district. Unbeknownst to Brownie the division's officers bemoaned the shortages of men and the AEF's failure to develop a policy of returning soldiers, who had recovered from their wounds, to their units.[6]

The occupation duty proved a trying time. The soldiers wanted to return home to civilian life. Officers struggled to maintain discipline when most of the doughboys viewed their job as done. Pershing eventually relaxed some rules and encouraged the development of sports and educational programs to keep the men occupied. One of the biggest problems was the men's desire to fraternize with the local population. Although officially prohibited, the men could not resist. Unfortunately, the once-controlled venereal disease rates spiraled out of hand.[7] The fight against the diseases only came to an end when the division completed its occupation duty at the end of March.

JANUARY 2, 1919 (St. Nazaire)

Dearest Marty,

You see I've moved again after a stay of nearly two months in Angers. I'm not kicking on moving either especially since it's some nearer home here. I landed here on the first of November in 1917 and returned on Jan. 1, 1919 so there's fourteen months in France. And I don't know how many more tho I'm hoping it's not even one.

My Service Record has never turned up but finally they've decided to send us back without them, so here we are awaiting our turn. In some ways I was sorry to leave Angers as it was the best place I ever lived in France. St. Nazaire is quite a town too but we are stationed quite a way out and it's much muddier or more muddy and dirtier than Angers. About eight hundred casuals came along with me on box-cars of course and the ride took us about nine hours. Not very swift! . . .

I managed to get a little money during the latter part of my stay in Angers. Perhaps that's why I enjoyed myself there and perhaps that's why I didn't write more often. It does make it convenient to have some money and I should be able to vouch for that since August pay was the last I drew. That seems a long while ago now Marty. I often wonder what has been going on at home since I last heard. . . .

It will be useless for you to write me any more Marty till I give you an address to write to. I guess it has been useless for the last two months but I hated to say stop writing when there was a chance of my getting your letters. As it is now I ought to leave here for the States soon. Perhaps I'll even beat this letter across. I wish so. There are so many rumors of when we leave floating around that no one knows anything for sure. I never figure on leaving till I go so I'm never worried about it. We have nothing to do only rest and sleep but that's plenty for a soldier.

JANUARY 19, 1919

Now I have hopes of coming home soon. Are you tired of listening to my hopes? I've been hoping and writing about it since last Thanksgiving and it seems as if you must be tired of such letters. Anyway everything looks now as if I would leave this week. I am a casual of course and go to New York state since I enlisted there and last night I was put into a N.Y. Casual Co. There will be lots to do this week, inspections etc. but if everyone helps out it won't take so long to finish them all. I think we are to get all our back pay before we leave which for me means from Sept. to Dec. inclusive. I ought to be happy but after having waited for two months it's hard to be elated.

Of course I've no notion of what will happen to us when we reach New York but it can't be so very long then to the time we'll be mustered out. I don't expect to be overjoyed by the trip across but I sure am overjoyed at the prospect of our destination. And so Marty I ought to be home soon, and then I can see you. Are you going to ask me up? You'd better or I'll have to come without being asked. It's so long since I heard from you and I want to ask you so many things I'm afraid we'll talk for two weeks steady.

This seems too good to be true to be writing you from this side of the pond.

Surely I've been away long enough so that I ought to appreciate the U.S. & I do. I'm so glad to be back and there's so many things to see and do that I hardly know what to do first. The thing that struck me first when we got on the streets was to hear the children speak English. I couldn't make it seem natural at first. Then everything is so nice and clean, the civilians so well dressed. I know nothing about the prices of things but just the fact that everything is so plentiful over here. All one has to do is look into the shop windows and he'd know he was in America. Big apples and oranges, anything like that. Really Marty, I just began to live again when I passed down the streets here.

I'm sure raving on but I've not been here long enough to really appreciate my good luck yet. We landed here at Newport News about 10 a.m. yesterday having been 13 days crossing. We came by the Southern Route on the U.S.S. *Rijndam.* Then we were marched out here to Camp Hill and were put in the best barracks I've seen since Slocum. We have heaters and baths and good eats. They are fixing up the payroll, sterilizing all our clothes etc. and soon we'll be on our way to Camp Upton, L.I. [Long Island]. They say that's the demobilization camp for N.Y. State. Today the Red Cross furnished ice cream for all the guys who landed yesterday. We had it for dinner—all we wanted.

I'm crazy to get home but think that I'll be mustered out first. Anyway I can easily stand a little waiting here. Things come so slow in the Army that a month seems a short time to wait. I really expect to be out very soon now, tho. Then there'll be my first trip to see you, Marty. . . . It seems to me as tho you had changed but perhaps that's because I havn't heard from you in so long. But no doubt I am different too or seem so anyway. We'll soon be able to satisfy our minds now Marty. . . . And soon it's going to be the nice time of year. I'm too happy it seems and I've such memories of "our" last summer. But let's wait.

FEBRUARY 16, 1919

I'm on Long Island again and before another week I'll be home.

Yesterday I had a letter from home—the first one from anyone since I left the 117th. Naturally it was full of surprises. So many things had happened that I didn't know of.

For some time I had been thinking that perhaps you didn't live in East Morris any more. The last letters you wrote me read as tho you might not be there long. I have been wishing for one letter cause then it would be so much easier to write back. If you have received all the letters I sent you, you'll know I must be tired of writing about what happened to "I". It's a consolation that we won't have to write much longer. . . .

Probably the next time you hear from me will be by telephone. In a few days now, I hope. Good-bye Marty and don't forget.

Your own,
Brownie

A little over a month after Brownie returned to the United States, the 42nd Division left the Rhine and began its trip home. Traveling on different ships, the various units in the division arrived in the United States in late April and early May and returned to their originating states. The remainder of the AEF returned home by the end of August. In November 1918 the AEF's strength was 1,971,000. When Pershing left France in August 1919, the AEF had been disbanded and there were roughly 12,000 men that composed the American forces in Germany. These forces remained there until January 1923.[8]

The AEF played a vital role in the Allies' ultimate victory on the western front. The addition of American soldiers and supplies gave the Allies the necessary advantage to force the Central powers' surrender. Taken together, the American, British, French, and other Allied forces presented Germany and its allies with an insurmountable obstacle. Their efforts came with a cost, as 7,485,000 men and women died. The United States only experienced a small percentage of those losses, yet World War I still remains the third costliest war in American history, only behind the Civil War and World War II. More than 2 million doughboys ultimately served in the AEF, and almost 1.4 million served at the front. More than 320,000 were killed or wounded. Brownie's 42nd Division suffered more than 14,000 casualties, including over 900 in his engineering regiment.[9]

FEBRUARY 24, 1919

Dearest Marty,

. . . I've been wanting to write you ever since I left you yesterday
afternoon. I just can't help it Marty, I've got it bad. That sounds as
tho I were writing someone else but weno. I feel funny every time I
think of you. Much worse than when I was up with you. I want you
too much Marty—It hurts—some—not unpleasant. Don't ever let
me lose you. I'm not "nutty" if I am writing this way. Just trying to
tell you something that can't be expressed. Often I've wanted to
write and tell you how much I love you Marty. Sometime I'll write
9000 pages full of it—for a starter. I must see you again soon for
it seems as tho I hadn't started to tell you things yet. And, tho
I'm sure of you, sometimes I imagine that I'm not sure. You'll
think I'm in a terrible state and I guess I am—in love plus. Please
forgive me if you don't approve of such letters Marty. If you say so
I'll never do it again. . . .

I had a wonderful time, you're the nicest girl in the world.

MARCH 7, 1919

. . . To-day I'm doing nothing as usual and last night was mostly
spent thinking of you. Really I hardly slept at all. I don't mean to
do it any more tho you're sure worth thinking about. And when
I'm at your house I can sleep fine. Perhaps that is because you are
near or it might be that I'm sleepy. I wonder. Do you still want to
marry me Marty? I'm going to ask you that a million times before
we really are married. If you get too tired of hearing me ask it
we'll be married right off. Then I'd change it and ask if you were
still glad you did. I'll try not to be tiresome but I might be. After
living to-gether for a year will things seem different and if so in
what way? Let's love all the more, Marty, I want to.

. . . Let's love always and always plus. Don't forget me Marty,
I'm coming up to see you at least once more.

> Eldred or Brownie or Geo.
> Which shall it be?

Brownie was officially discharged from the army on February 18, 1919 and went to see Marty as soon as he could.[10] Un-

11. George Browne and Martha Johnson on their wedding day in August 1919. Courtesy of Janet Hansen.

fortunately, the written record of their relationship came to a close with Brownie's March 7 letter. Their big event after his homecoming was planning their wedding. They were married at Marty's home in East Morris, Connecticut, on August 9, 1919.[11] After their wedding they moved to Waterbury.[12] Brownie worked as a civil engineer for the City of Waterbury while Marty stayed at home collecting antiques and gardening.[13] Although they

12. George and Martha Browne in the late 1960s. Courtesy of Janet Hansen.

evidently wanted children they never were able to have any. They eventually retired to Morris, where Brownie died on September 12, 1971. Marty lived another 18 years before passing away on October 16, 1989.[14]

Brownie and Marty's deaths closed a chapter in American history. In the early twenty-first century, there are very few Americans who can remember the events of that era. However, Brownie's letters provide an enduring link to the past and a portrait of what life was like for an average American doughboy during World War I. They also show how wartime separations can affect relationships. Just like their country, Brownie and Marty persevered through the difficult times and emerged from the war ready for a new beginning.

Composition of the Rainbow Division

Tasker H. Bliss to Commanding Generals, All Departments, August 1, 1917, UNLA, RDC, World War I, Box 1, Folder 9, 1.

Original State Unit	Organization within the 42nd Division
Alabama—4th Infantry Regiment	167th Infantry Regiment
California—1st Separate Engineer Battalion	2nd Battalion, 117th Engineers Regiment
Colorado—1st Field Hospital Company	3rd Field Hospital Company, 117th Sanitary Train
District of Columbia—1st Field Hospital Company	1st Field Hospital, 117th Sanitary Train
Georgia—B, C, and F Companies, 2nd Infantry	151st Machine Gun Battalion
Indiana—1st Field Artillery	150th Field Artillery Regiment
Illinois—1st Field Artillery	149th Field Artillery Regiment
Kansas—1st Ammunition Train	117th Ammunition Train
Iowa—3rd Infantry Regiment	168th Infantry Regiment
Louisiana—2nd Separate Cavalry Troop	Divisional Headquarters Cavalry Troop
Maryland—3rd and 4th Coast Artillery Companies	117th Trench Mortar Company

Michigan—1st Ambulance Company	1st Ambulance Company, 117th Sanitary Train
Minnesota—1st Field Artillery	151st Field Artillery Regiment
Missouri—1st Field Signal Battalion	117th Field Signal Battalion
Nebraska—1st Field Hospital Company	2nd Field Hospital Company, 117th Sanitary Train
New Jersey—1st Ambulance Company	2nd Ambulance Company, 117th Sanitary Train
New York—69th Infantry	165th Infantry Regiment
North Carolina—Engineer Train	117th Engineers Train
Ohio—4th Infantry Regiment	166th Infantry Regiment
Oklahoma—1st Ambulance Company	4th Ambulance Company, 117th Sanitary Train
Oregon—1st Field Hospital Company	4th Field Hospital Company, 117th Sanitary Train
Pennsylvania—3rd Battalion, 4th Infantry	149th Machine Gun Battalion Regiment
South Carolina—1st Separate Engineer Battalion	1st Battalion, 117th Engineers Regiment
Tennessee—1st Ambulance Company	3rd Ambulance Company, 117th Sanitary Train
Texas—Supply Train	117th Supply Train
Virginia—Coast Artillery Corps	117th Headquarters Train and Military Police
Wisconsin—E, F, and G Companies, 2nd Infantry	150th Machine Gun Battalion

Introduction

1. State of Connecticut Military Census for George E. Browne, March 8, 1917, Connecticut State Library and Archives, Hartford CT, Record Group 29 (hereafter RG)—Records of the Military Census, 1. See also "Wolcott," *Waterbury Republican*, February 23, 1919, 5.

2. Biographical Sketch of Martha Ingersoll Johnson, July 16, 1976, in author's possession. Marty was a schoolteacher in East Morris from 1915 to 1919. See Weik, "*One Hundred Years*," 68.

3. See for example Leed, *No Man's Land*, xi–xii. Leed argues that "the war contributed to the character of the age by altering the status, expectations, and character of participants."

4. The basic pay of a private, Brownie rank when he joined the army, was $30 a month. See Chambers, *To Raise an Army*, 167. For all enlisted men in World War I, the average basic pay was $34.75 per month and for all officers it was $178.42. See *U.S. Bureau of the Census, Statistical History of the United States*, 1140.

5. For a description of Fort Slocum, see *Order of Battle*, vol. 3, *Zone of the Interior*, pt. 2, *Territorial Departments*, 790.

6. Bantam is a small town approximately twenty-two miles from Waterbury and only a few miles from Marty's home in Morris. Bantam Lake provided a vacation spot for many citizens of Waterbury, and Marty and Brownie spent the Fourth of July weekend with her family there before he formally enlisted.

7. All letters from George Browne to Martha Johnson are in the author's possession.

8. For a good, yet brief introduction to the causes of World War I, see Turner, *Origins of the First World War*.

9. There are many excellent overall histories of World War I. Among the best are Gilbert, *First World War: A Complete History*; Keegan, *First*

World War; and Tucker, *Great War*. For the best study of trench warfare in general, see Ellis, *Eye-Deep in Hell*.

10. The best overview of Woodrow Wilson's presidency is Clements, *Presidency of Woodrow Wilson*. For studies of American neutrality and why the United States ultimately declared war, see Burk, *Britain, America and the Sinews of War*; Cooper, *Vanity of Power*; Gregory, *Origins of American Intervention*); Link, *Woodrow Wilson*; May, *World War and American Isolation*; and Tuchman, *Zimmermann Telegram*.

11. For a detailed description of the country's mood in early 1917, see Kennedy, *Over There: First World War*, 3–44.

12. Clements, *Presidency of Woodrow Wilson*, 137–41.

13. Studies that examine the overall American war effort at home and abroad include Ferrell, *Woodrow Wilson and World War I*; Keene, *United States in the First World War*; Kennedy, *Over There: First World War*; and Ziegler, *America's Great War*. A excellent book that examines how World War I influenced the development of the United States later in the twentieth century is Keene, *Doughboys, the Great War*.

14. The best studies include Coffman, *War to End All Wars*; Stallings, *Doughboys: Story*; and Farwell, *Over There: United States*. Other studies of American military involvement in the war include Eisenhower, *Yanks*; Freidel, *Over There: Story*; Harries and Harries, *Last Days of Innocence*; Hallas, *Doughboy War*; and Mead, *Doughboys: America*.

1. Mobilization and Training

1. Various factors and issues motivated soldiers from the United States and other countries to serve and fight. In a recent study of American soldiers in the twentieth century, Peter Kindsvatter argues, "Primary-group cohesion and belief in cause and country were . . . an essential combination, with unit esprit a supplementary motivator." Kindsvatter, *American Soldiers*, 134. See also Linderman, *Embattled Courage* and *World Within War*; Lynn, *Bayonets of the Republic*; and McPherson, *For Cause and Comrades*.

2. See Kreidberg and Henry, *History of Military Mobilization*, 221–22; and Farwell, *Over There: United States*, 37. Another way to look at the military's level of unpreparedness is that in 1915 there was one regular army soldier for every 1,150 inhabitants of the United States. In Great Britain, there was one for every 205, in Germany one for every 70, and in France one for every 50. See Dickinson, *Building of an Army*, 10.

3. Farwell, *Over There: United States*, 246. A closer look at the expansion reveals that from March 1917 to November 1918, the number of infantry and machine gunners increased from 85,000 to 974,000, engineers from 3,000 to 394,000, artillerymen from 9,000 to 389,000,

and medical support from 7,000 to 300,000. See Dickinson, *Building of an Army*, 118–19.

4. Johnson and Hillman, *Soissons*, xvi. See also Hamburger, *Learning Lessons*, 9; Mead, *Doughboys: America*, 95; and Victory, "Soldier Making," 62, 105.

5. See Nenninger, "American Military Effectiveness," 117–18; Abrahamson, *America Arms*, 158; Rainey, "Questionable Training," 90; Cooper, *Rise of the National Guard*, 167; and Seymour, *Woodrow Wilson and the World War*, 117.

6. See Trask, AEF *and Coalition Warmaking*, 11; and Braim, *Test of Battle*, 20.

7. See Kreidberg and Henry, *History of Military Mobilization*, 311, 314, 318; Bond and Sherrill, *America in the World War*, 50; Farwell, *Over There: United States*, 54; Crowell and Wilson, *How America Went to War*, 71; Fortescue, "Training the New Armies of Liberty," 421–37; and Showalter, "America's New Soldier Cities," 438–76.

8. Cooke, *Rainbow Division*, 9.

9. See Braim, *Test of Battle*, 38; Coffman, *War to End All Wars*, 38–42; Paschall, *Defeat of Imperial Germany*, 52; and Stallings, *Doughboys: Story*, 25.

10. Farwell, *Over There: United States*, 54.

11. Bond and Sherrill, *America in the World War*, 96–98.

12. Camp Mills was located on Long Island, New York. For a description, see *Order of Battle*, vol. 3, pt. 2, 753–54.

13. Kindsvatter, *American Soldiers*, xix.

14. Floyd Rinehart, "Veteran Recalls Days of the Rainbow Division," University of Nebraska–Lincoln Love Library (hereafter UNLA), Rainbow Division Collection (hereafter RDC), Rainbow Division Veterans' Association Collection (hereafter RDVA), RDVA Chapters, Box 6, Folder 2, no page.

15. "War Victory Tops in Private's Mind," *Rainbow Reveille* 2, no. 17 (December 16, 1943), UNLA, RDC, RDVA, RDVA Chapters, Box 6, Oversize Folder 6.

16. Quoted in Hallas, *Doughboy War*, 9.

17. "Manhood of Nation Will Register Today," *Charleston News and Courier*, June 5, 1917, 1.

18. "What We're Fighting For," *Stars and Stripes*, March 13, 1918, 1. The appeal of national pride could also be seen in the drive to sell Liberty Bonds. One advertisement read, "Above all, if you appreciate the liberty that your country gives to you and yours, if you believe it worth while that these United States shall continue to exist in honor and in peace, you should at least lend your money to that cause as freely

as others are dedicating their lives." See "Liberty War Bonds," *Charleston News and Courier,* June 1, 1917, 7.

19. The best studies of the World War I draft are Chambers, *To Raise an Army;* and Baldwin, "American Enlisted Man."

20. Kreidberg and Henry, *History of Military Mobilization,* 244–77; Dickinson, *Building of an Army,* 97–98; Coffman, *War to End All Wars,* 28–29; Victory, "Soldier Making," 17; and Chambers, *To Raise an Army,* 179–204.

21. Farwell, *Over There: United States,* 61. These figures are in line with the population as a whole as only 14.5 and 15.1 percent of seventeen-year-olds received high-school diplomas in 1917 and 1918, respectively. *U.S. Bureau of the Census, Statistical History of the United States,* 379. See also Victory, "Soldier Making," 2.

22. Farwell, *Over There: United States,* 51.

23. State of Connecticut Military Census for George E. Browne, March 8, 1917, Connecticut State Library and Archives, Hartford CT, RG 29—Records of the Military Census, 1. In early 1917 in preparation for the possibility of United States entering the war, Connecticut took a census of all men over the age of sixteen. Brownie was one of slightly more than 500,000 men who registered. See library's Web site at http://www.cslib.org/milcens.htm for information on the census.

24. Baldwin, "American Enlisted Man," 64.

25. See Dickinson, *Building of an Army,* 85; and *United States Army in the World War,* vol. 1, *Organization of the American Expeditionary Forces,* 115. The average division was broken down as follows: two brigades each containing two infantry regiments and a machine gun battalion (approximately 8,400 men per brigade); regiments consisted of three battalions and a machine gun company (approximately 4,000 men); battalions contained four companies (approximately 1,000 men); companies had four platoons (approximately 250 men); platoons were broken into seven squads (56 men); and squads were made up of eight men. In addition there were separate specialized units like the artillery and engineers.

26. Tasker H. Bliss to Commanding Generals, All Departments, August 1, 1917, UNLA, RDC, World War I, Box 1, Folder 9, 1.

27. Reilly, *Americans All,* 5–6, 26–29.

28. Cooke, *Rainbow Division,* 4.

29. "Engineers Urged to Enlist Quickly," *Charleston News and Courier,* May 10, 1917, 6. For the a more complete discussion of the involvement of South Carolina troops in the Rainbow Division, see Snead, "South Carolina Engineers."

30. "History of the 117th Engineers, Story of Training and Fighting,"

Marion Star, March 12, 1919, 1; and "Raising Two Companies," ibid., May 16, 1917, 1.

31. "Johnson's Engineers Have Gone to Greenville Camp," *Marion Star*, August 22, 1917, 1.

32. "Company A Assembles Here on July 25th for 2 Weeks," *Marion Star*, July 18, 1917, 1.

33. "Engineers Leave Sevier Tomorrow," *Charleston News and Courier*, August 27, 1917, 1; "Carolinians Reach Camp," ibid., September 1, 1917, 1; "Engineers Leave for Long Island," *The State*, August 29, 1917, 1; and "History of the 117th Engineers," *Marion Star*, March 12, 1919, 1.

34. Cooke, *Rainbow Division*, 5. MacArthur rose to the rank of brigadier general later in the war.

35. Sadler, *California Rainbow Memories*, 20.

36. Cooke, *Rainbow Division*, 18. The soldiers were supposed to be allotted one overcoat, one poncho, one waist belt, one pair leggings, one service hat, two shirts, two pair of shoes, two coats, two pants, three undershirts, three changes of underwear, and five pairs of socks. See Memorandum, September 12, 1917, National Archives of the United States, College Park, Maryland (hereafter NA), RG 120, World War I, Organizational Records, 42nd Division, Box 25, Folder—84th Infantry Brigade, Historical Data 1917, 1.

37. Although this did not happen that often, soldiers in the regular army units were sometimes assigned to National Guard divisions to fill more specialized needs.

38. The YMCA provided services for the soldiers throughout the war. For descriptions of the YMCA during the war, see Lancaster, *Serving the U.S. Armed Forces*, 46–84; and Taft et al., *Service with Fighting Men*.

39. General Orders No. 6, September 8, 1917, NA, RG 120, World War I, Organizational Records, 42nd Division, Box 25, Folder—84th Infantry Brigade, Historical Data 1917, 4. For descriptions of these diseases and the vaccines for them, see Siler, *Medical Department*, 15–60, 357–86; and Bayne-Jones, *Evolution of Preventive Medicine*, 151.

40. Memorandum, September 10, 1917, NA, RG 120, World War I, Organizational Records, 42nd Division, Box 25, Folder—84th Infantry Brigade, Historical Data 1917, 1.

41. General Orders No. 6, September 8, 1917, NA, RG 120, World War I, Organizational Records, 42nd Division, Box 25, Folder—84th Infantry Brigade, Historical Data 1917, 2.

42. General Orders No. 6, September 8, 1917NA, RG 120, World War I, Organizational Records, 42nd Division, Box 25, Folder—84th Infantry Brigade, Historical Data 1917, 3.

43. Along with "doughboy", "Sammie" was a common nickname for American soldiers in World War I. See Mead, *Doughboys: America*, 66–68.

44. General Orders No. 5 (MacArthur), September 8, 1917, NA, RG 120, World War I, Organizational Records, 42nd Division, Box 25, Folder—84th Infantry Brigade, Historical Data 1917, 1–2.

45. Taber, *Story of the 168th Infantry*, vol. 1, 11.

46. See General Orders No. 5 (MacArthur), September 8, 1917, NA, RG 120, World War I, Organizational Records, 42nd Division, Box 25, Folder—84th Infantry Brigade, Historical Data 1917, 1; General Orders No. 5, September 7, 1917, ibid., Box 18, Folder—42nd Division—Training Program 1917, 1–3; and General Orders No. 5 (MacArthur), September 18, 1917, ibid., Box 25, Folder—84th Infantry Brigade—Historical Data 1917, 1–2.

47. Cooke, *Rainbow Division*, 17.

48. Reilly, *Americans All*, 32.

49. Personal Experiences, Observations, and Incidents Compiled from Notes, Orders, Messages and Memory of Isaac G. Walker, Former First Lieutenant Company A, 151st Machine Gun Battalion, 42nd Division, Archives, United States Army Military History Institute, Carlisle Barracks PA (hereafter USAMHI), World War I Military History Surveys, 42nd Division, 84th Infantry Brigade, Folder—Isaac G. Walker, Co. A, 151st Machine Gun Battalion, World War I Survey, 1. See also Collins, *Minnesota in the World War*, 19–20; and William E. Gilmore, History of the Headquarters Company, 149th Field Artillery, USAMHI, Henry J. Reilly Papers, Box 46, Folder—Hdqtrs. Co., 149th FA, 27.

50. Stansbury, *Maryland's 117th Trench Mortar Battery*, 9.

51. Letter to My Dear Little Sister [Doris Leonard], September 28, 1917, USAMHI, Henry J. Reilly Papers, Box 46, Box 42nd Division, 84th Infantry Brigade, Folder—8179, Leonard, Rollyn E., 12.

52. Walt Michael to Ray and Barbara, October 1, 1917, UNLA, RDC, RDVA Papers, Individual Papers, Box 11, Folder 1, 1.

53. General Orders No. 7, September 9, 1917, NA, RG 120, World War I, Organizational Records, 42nd Division, Box 20, Folder—42nd Division General Orders (1917, 1918), 1; and General Orders No. 4 (MacArthur), September 6, 1917, ibid., Box 25, Folder—84th Infantry Brigade, Historical Data—1917, 1.

54. Cooke, *Rainbow Division*, 15.

55. "Coon" was a derogatory term used to describe black Americans.

56. "Wop" was a slang term, often seen as derogatory, used to describe Italians. There were approximately 500,000 recent immigrants to the United States in the AEF representing forty-six different countries by the end of the war. See Gentile, *Americans All!*, 3.

57. Jake's full name was Jacob Kopishpo. He was later assigned to Company E, 117th Engineers.

58. "L" was an elevated local train.

59. Brownie uses this abbreviation quite a bit. It seems to stand for "You and I know."

60. While it is unclear what happened on their last night together, it becomes evident later that Brownie, at some point, did ask Marty to marry him.

61. Brownie had evidently received a pass and been able to visit Marty.

62. Brownie had visited Marty while on a pass.

63. This was the last pass Brownie received before going overseas.

64. Browne to Johnson, August 12, 1917, in author's possession.

2. From the States to France

1. Kreidberg and Henry, *History of Military Mobilization*, 324.

2. Quoted in Crowell and Wilson, *How America Went to War*, 311.

3. Freidel, *Over There: Story*, 16.

4. See Frothingham, *American Reinforcement*, 109; Hurley, *Bridge to France*, 39; Crowell and Wilson, *How America Went to War*, 417, 603–20; and Kreidberg and Henry, *History of Military Mobilization*, 336.

5. See Kreidberg and Henry, *History of Military Mobilization*, 335; Bond and Sherrill, *America in the World War*, 57; and Frothingham, *American Reinforcement*, 258.

6. See Tompkins, *Story of the Rainbow Division*, 17; Sadler, *California Rainbow Memories*, 20–22; and Memorandum: Embarkation Duties On Board Transport and Disembarkation, October 15, 1917, NA, RG 120, World War I Organizational Records, 42nd Division, Box 25, Folder— 84th Infantry Brigade, Historical Data 1917, 4.

7. See Bartlet T. Bent Diary, England, 1918–19, Connecticut Historical Society, Hartford CT, 1; and Memorandum for Commanding Officer and Supply Officer, October 14, 1917, NA, RG 120, World War I, Organizational Records, 42nd Division, Box 4, Folder—no name, 2.

8. Wilbur C. Peterson, "Memories of Rainbow," UNLA, RDVA Papers, World War I, Box 2, Folder 14, 5–6.

9. Tompkins, *Story of the Rainbow Division*, 18.

10. Commanding General, 84th Brigade, 42nd Division, November 5, 1917, NA, RG 120, World War I, Organizational Records, 42nd Division, Box 25, Folder—84th Infantry Brigade, Historical Data 1917, 1.

11. Collins, *Minnesota in the World War*, 21–22.

12. Cooke, *Rainbow Division*, 19. See also William E. Gilmore, History of the Headquarters Company, 149th First Artillery, USAMHI, Henry J. Reilly Papers, Box 46, Folder—Hdqtrs. Co., 149th FA, 34; and Frank T. Kolar, "So Far All In: Diary of a Common Soldier," UNLA, RDC, RDVA Papers, Individual Papers, Box 7, Folder 4, 3.

13. Benjamin Leo Bory, Army Service Experiences Questionnaire,

USAMHI, World War I Military History Surveys, Box 42nd Division #3, 67th Field Artillery Brigade, Folder—WWI—5996, Bory, Benjamin L., 5.

14. C.O. Ambulance Section, 117th Sanitary Train to Commanding General, 84th Infantry Brigade, October 20, 1917, NA, RG 120, World War I, Organizational Records, 42nd Division, Box 25, Folder—84th Infantry Brigade, Historical Data 1917, 1.

15. Ned W. Harden, "Pickaway County in the Rainbow (Part I)," *Pickaway Quarterly*, Winter 1985, UNLA, RDC, RDVA Papers, World War I, Box 2, Folder 8, 20.

16. Diary of Signal Platoon, Headquarters Co., 166th Infantry, 42nd Rainbow Division, UNLA, RDC, RDVA Papers, World War I, Box 2, Folder 7, 1.

17. War Diary of W. G. Hudson, 1917–1918, Connecticut Historical Society, Hartford CT, 2. See also Hallas, *Doughboy War*, 33.

18. Joseph, *WW I Diary of Pvt. Emile M. Calhoun*, 24–25.

19. Young, *Hugh Young*, 308–9.

20. Stallings, *Doughboys: Story*, 181. The three main venereal diseases were gonorrhea, chancroid, and syphilis. See Walker, *Venereal Disease*, 134–48. In the summer of 1917, there were twenty-three thousand British soldiers in hospitals with venereal diseases and the French had suffered more than a million cases of syphilis and gonorrhea. Smythe, "Venereal Disease: The AEF's Experience," 65.

21. William Finch, Army Service Experiences Questionnaire, USAMHI, World War I Military History Surveys, Box 42nd Division #3, 67th Field Artillery Brigade, Folder—WWI—2014, Finch, William, 6.

22. Pershing expressed concerns with the potential problems of venereal diseases as early as July 1917. In an order on July 2, Pershing claimed, "A soldier who contracts a venereal disease not only suffers permanent injury, but renders himself inefficient as a soldier and becomes an incumbrance to the Army. He fails in his duty to his country and to his comrades." General Order No. 6, July 2, 1917, in Walker, *Venereal Disease*, 58. For copies of Pershing's orders pertaining to venereal diseases throughout the war, see Walker, *Venereal Disease*, 58–74.

23. Young, *Hugh Young*, 307.

24. Memorandum to Regimental Commanders, November 3, 1917, NA, RG 120, World War I, Organizational Records, 42nd Division, Box 36, Folder—67th FA Brig. (A.G.) Memos (1917, 1918), 1.

25. Hallas, *Doughboy War*, 42–43. For an interesting perspective on the AEF's portrayal of women, see Zeiger, *In Uncle Sam's Service*, 143–45.

26. Young, *Hugh Young*, 30.

27. Frank T. Kolar, "So Far All In: Diary of a Common Soldier," UNLA, RDC, RDVA Papers, Individual Papers, Box 7, Folder 4, 7.

28. Young, *Hugh Young*, 308–9. Laurence Stallings presents one horrifying case where eight American soldiers who used the same prostitute in an assembly line–like fashion contracted syphilis. See Stallings, *Doughboys: Story*, 179–80. Dr. George Walker recalled that "during a period of ten days at St. Nazaire, an official French report stated that 60 women in four houses of prostitution served 15,000 Americans, or 25 men per day per woman." Walker, *Venereal Disease*, 84.

29. Young, *Hugh Young*, 306.

30. General Orders No. 15, November 18, 1917, NA, RG 120, World War I, Organizational Records, 42nd Division, Box 20, Folder—42nd Division, General Orders (1917, 1918), 1.

31. See General Orders No. 15, November 18, 1917, NA, RG 120, World War I, Organizational Records, 42nd Division, Box 20, Folder—42nd Division, General Orders (1917, 1918), 1.; Special Order No. 30, November 12, 1917, ibid., Box 17, Folder—42nd Division, G-4 Orders, 1; and Young, *Hugh Young*, 310–12.

32. General Orders No. 15, November 18, 1917, NA, RG 120, World War I, Organizational Records, 42nd Division, Box 20, Folder—42nd Division, General Orders (1917, 1918), 1.

33. Evans, *American Voices of World War I*, 11.

34. Farwell, *Over There: United States*, 142. Argyrol is an organic silver salt that was known to be effective against gonorrhea. Calomel is the common name for mercuric chloride, which is commonly used as a disinfectant. For a medical description of the procedure used to prevent the spread of venereal diseases within hours of a soldier's exposure, see Walker, *Venereal Disease*, 10–13. For a medical description of the treatment of soldiers who actually contracted venereal diseases, see Walker, *Venereal Disease*, 116–19.

35. See Baldwin, "American Enlisted Man," 214; and Siler, *Medical Department*, 263–69.

36. The President du Conseil, Minister of War (Clemenceau to General Chief of the French Mission, AEF), February 17, 1918, in Walker, *Venereal Disease*, 95.

37. Walker, *Venereal Disease*, 84.

38. See Young, *Hugh Young*, 312; and Farwell, *Over There: United States*, 147. Fewer than one thousand American soldiers were in the hospital in the fall of 1918 because of venereal diseases. Smythe, "Venereal Disease: The AEF's Experience," 73.

39. Ettinger and Ettinger, *Doughboy with the Fighting Sixty-ninth*, 59.

40. War Diary of W. G. Hudson, 1917–1918, Connecticut Historical Society, Hartford CT, 3.

41. Quoted in Sadler, *California Rainbow Memories*, 23.

42. Wilbur C. Peterson, "Memories of Rainbow," UNLA, RDVA Papers, World War I, Box 2, Folder 14, 10.

43. Memorandum to Regimental Commanders, November 3, 1917, NA, RG 120, World War I, Organizational Records, 42nd Division, Box 36, Folder—67th FA Brig. (A.G.) Memos (1917, 1918), 1.

44. Triplet , *A Youth in the Meuse-Argonne*, 39.

45. For Pershing's views on the National Guard, see Johnson and Hillman, *Soissons*, 21.

46. See Bridges, "Through the Fire," 2, 27; *United States Army in the World War*, vol. 3, *Training and Use of American Units with the British and French*, 665–70; and Cooke, *Rainbow Division*, 20.

47. Savine Rondilone was a private in Company A, 117th Engineers. See Johnson, *Roster of the Rainbow Division*, 75.

48. Alida was a family friend.

49. Cooties are body lice.

50. See "History of the 117th Engineers Story of Training and Fighting," *Marion Star*, March 12, 1919, 1; and 242-10.7: Station List, *United States Army in the World War*, vol. 3, 665.

51. Pershing to Pétain, January 6, 1918, in *United States Army in the World War*, vol. 3, 261.

52. General Orders No. 22, December 22, 1917, NA, RG 120, World War I, Organizational Records, 42nd Division, Box 8, Folder—Division G.O. Supplementary F.O.s, 11.

53. Freidel, *Over There: Story*, 50.

54. Wolf, *Brief History of the Rainbow Division*, 8.

55. Tompkins, *Story of the Rainbow*, 25. See also Jas. A. Webb, "Painting the Rainbow," *Army and Navy Record*, April 1920, 34; and Lieutenant Hensey, Chapter 3—Thanksgiving and Christmas, USAMHI, Henry J. Reilly Papers, Box 43, Folder—Chapter 4—Thanksgiving and Christmas 1917, 6.

56. Diary of Signal Platoon, Headquarters Co., 166th Infantry, 42nd Rainbow Division, UNLA, RDC, RDVA Papers, World War I, Box 2, Folder 7, 2.

57. Freidel, *Over There: Story*, 94.

58. Quoted in Sadler, *California Rainbow Memories*, 23. See also Tompkins, *Story of the Rainbow*, 19.

59. Corey, "Cooties and Courage," 495–97.

60. Quoted in Freidel, *Over There: Story*, 50.

61. Stansbury, *Maryland's 117th Trench Mortar Battery*, 26–27.

62. See "With the Rainbow Division in France," 8. The uniform for field service included a steel helmet, overcoat, woolen service coat, woolen service breeches, flannel shirt, woolen undershirt, woolen un-

derwear, heavy woolen socks, woolen gloves, wrapped puttees, hob-nailed trench shoes, two identification tags, a small box respirator, and a French gas mask. Each soldier was supposed to also carry in his pack a sweater, blanket, poncho, razor, comb, bar of soap, three pairs of heavy woolen socks, woolen underwear, woolen undershirt, flannel shirt, toothbrush, towel cap, two days rations, and one hundred rounds of ammunition. Confidential Memorandum No. 33, February 9, 1918, NA, RG 120, World War I, Organizational Records, 42nd Division, Box 1, Folder—42nd Division GA-1 and Administration Memos (numbered Jan.), 1.

63. Quoted in Freidel, *Over There: Story*, 58.

64. "Sugar Costs $1.00 a Pound in France," *Charleston News and Courier*, June 16, 1918, 10.

65. Evans, *American Voices*, 29.

66. Corey, "Cooties and Courage," 500, 509.

67. J. Slavney, "Maryland's 117th Trench Mortar Battery in the World War 1917–1919," UNLA, RDC, RDVA Papers, World War I, Box 2, Folder 5, 7. Dr. Hugh Young reports that up to 75 percent of the 42nd Division was infected with lice in early 1918. See Young, *Hugh Young*, 338.

68. "The Coy and Playful Cootie," UNLA, RDC, RDVA Papers, World War I, Box 1, Folder 4.

69. "Delousing the Cootie," *Charleston News and Courier*, March 23, 1919, 10.

70. Memorandum, November 27, 1917, NA, RG 120, World War I, Organizational Records, 42nd Division, Box 1, Folder—42nd Division, G-1 Memos 1917, 1–4. For a description of these illnesses and diseases, see Shay, *Grateful Heart*, 180–89.

71. Transcript of Medical Detachment of the 117th Engineers, UNLA, RDC, RDVA Papers, World War I, Box 2, Folder 5, 3. In the 42nd Division, there were 110 medical officers, 25 dental officers, 20 veterinary officers, and 1,330 medical enlisted men. See "With the Rainbow Division in France."

72. For a description of gas masks, see Cooke, *Rainbow Division*, 86.

73. *United States Army in the World War*, vol. 1, 3. See Trask, AEF *and Coalition Warmaking*, 11–13, 176.

74. Minutes of the Conference Held at Compiegne, January 24, 1918, in *United States Army in the World War*, vol. 2, *Policy-Forming Documents of the American Expeditionary Forces*, 181. See also Vandiver, *Black Jack*, 694–96.

75. For Chief of Staff from Pershing, January 1, 1918, in *United States Army in the World War*, vol. 2, 132.

76. Memorandum, December 18, 1917, NA, RG 120, World War I, Organizational Records, 42nd Division, Box 1, Folder—42nd Division, GA-1 Memos 1917, 1.

77. See Paschall, *Defeat of Imperial Germany*, 168; Rainey, "Ambivalent Warfare," 35; and Johnson and Hillman, *Soissons*, 30–32, 145, 148.

78. Combat Instructions, September 5, 1918, *United States Army in the World War*, vol. 2, 491.

79. For critiques of Pershing's open warfare tactics, see Nenninger, "Tactical Dysfunction," 177; Rainey, "Ambivalent Warfare," 34–35; Rainey, "Questionable Training," 91; and Victory, "Soldier Making," 126,

80. Memorandum for the Chief of Staff, November 6, 1917, in *United States Army in the World War*, vol. 2, 68.

81. Stallings, *Doughboys: Story*, 28.

82. Program of Training for the 42nd Division, NA, RG 120, World War I, Organizational Records, 42nd Division, Box 18, Folder—42nd Division, Training Program 1917, 1. The application of these ideas to the entire AEF can be seen in the General Principles Governing the Training of Units of the American Expeditionary Forces, April 9, 1918, in *United States Army in the World War*, vol. 2, 296.

83. See Collins, *Minnesota in the World War*, 24; and U.S. Army, *Historical Report of the Chief Engineer*, 172.

84. See Weekly Training Programs, Fall 1917, NA, RG 120, World War I, Organizational Records, 42nd Division, Box 25, Folder—84th Infantry Brigade, Historical Data 1917, 1–9; and Program of Training for the 42nd Division, ibid., Box 18, Folder—42nd Division—Training Program 1917, 5.

85. Tompkins, *Story of the Rainbow*, 21.

86. Diary of Signal Platoon, Headquarters Co., 166th Infantry, 42nd Rainbow Division, UNLA, RDC, RDVA Papers, World War I, Box 2, Folder 7, 1.

87. Memorandum for the Commander-in-Chief, February 20, 1918, NA, RG 120, World War I Organizational Records, 42nd Division, Box 21, Folder—42nd Division, Inspection Reports 1918 (Feb. 21/18), 2–3.

88. Bond and Sherrill, *America in the World War*, 52.

89. Hendricks, *Combat and Construction*, 1. Each engineering company was supposed to consist of 256 men. Ideally, there were would be 6 officers, 25 sergeants, 40 corporals, 168 privates, and 17 with miscellaneous ranks. See Tables of Organization, Corps Troops, Series B, November 1, 1918, ibid., 318.

90. See Baker Report, July 26, 1917, in *United States Army in the World War*, vol. 1, 84–85; and the General Principles Governing the Training of Units of the American Expeditionary Forces, April 9, 1918, in *United States Army in the World War*, vol. 2, 309.

91. Parsons, *American Engineers in*, 38–39.

92. See U.S. Army, *Historical Report of the Chief Engineer*, 155; Memorandum to Chief Engineer, AEF, December 3, 1917, NA, RG 120, World War I, Organizational Records, 42nd Division, Box 40–117th Engineers Regiment, Folder—117th Engineers History, 1; and Memorandum to Chief Engineer, AEF, January 2, 1918, ibid., 1. See also *Order of Battle*, vol. 2, *American Expeditionary Forces*, 273.

93. Memorandum to Chief Engineer, AEF, February 3, 1918, NA, RG 120, World War I, Organizational Records, 42nd Division, Box 40–117th Engineers Regiment, Folder—117th Engineers History, 1.

94. "History of the 117th Engineers Story of Training and Fighting," *Marion Star*, March 19, 1919, 1.

95. Memorandum to Chief Engineer, AEF, March 3, 1918, NA, RG 120, World War I, Organizational Records, 42nd Division, Box 40–117th Engineers Regiment, Folder—117th Engineers History, 1.

96. See "History of the 117th Engineers Story of Training and Fighting," *Marion Star*, March 19, 1919, 1; and Memorandum for Chief of Training Section, February 14, 1918, NA, RG 120, World War I, Organizational Records, 42nd Division, Box 21, Folder—42nd Division, Inspection Reports (Feb. 21/18), 1–2.

97. The "Kaiser" was German leader Wilhelm II.

98. Ellis, *Eye-Deep in Hell*, 137–40.

99. The first American troops saw combat at Cambrai from November 20 to December 4, 1917, when three American engineer regiments provided the British support in stopping a German attack. See *United States Army in the World War*, vol. 1, 7.

3. Training and Action in a Quiet Sector

1. See American Battle Monuments Commission, *42nd Division*, 5; and Commanding General, 42nd Division to Commanding General, 1st Army Corps, December 21, 1918, UNLA, RDC, RDVA, World War I, Box 2, Folder 4, 1.

2. See *United States Army in the World War*, vol. 1, 10; and Freidel, *Over There: Story*, 97.

3. *United States Army in the World War*, vol. 1, 13.

4. Johnson and Hillman, *Soissons*, 24.

5. See American Battle Monuments Commission, *42nd Division*, 5, 12–13; Cooke, *Rainbow Division*, 70–76; and Reilly, *Americans All*, 224.

6. See Sadler, *California Rainbow Memories*, 29–30; and Cooke, *Rainbow Division*, 79.

7. This information came from the 42nd Division, Summary of Intelligence, February 21 to June 19, 1918. These reports can be found at UNLA, RDC, RDVA Papers, World War I.

8. Collins, *Minnesota in the War*, 33.

9. Ralph Clark was a friend from Connecticut.

10. Brownie often used the French term Boche to describe German soldiers.

11. Parsons, *American Engineers*, 318–42. Normally, the front trench was 80 to 200 yards in front of the support trench, which was between 200 and 500 yards in front of the reserve trench.

12. Quoted in Reilly, *Americans All*, 123.

13. Quoted in Reilly, *Americans All*, 478–79. See also "Engineers' Work Sped Doughboys Toward Victory," *Stars and Stripes*, May 2, 1919, 3.

14. Memorandum No. 130, May 25, 1918, NA, RG 120, World War I, Organizational Records, 42nd Division, Box 17, Folder—42nd Division, Ext. from Original Reports, 1.

15. Ettinger and Ettinger, *Doughboy with the Fighting Sixty-ninth*, 74.

16. Evans, *American Voices*, 54.

17. Collins, *Minnesota in the World War*, 36–37.

18. Parsons, *American Engineers*, 336.

19. Jack Warren Carrol, "Who Said Sunny France?" *Stars and Stripes*, May 24, 1918, 5.

20. Only on few occasions were Brownie's letters censored. Censors did not normally allow specific information about locations and distances to pass. While censorship was difficult for the soldiers, it was not an easy task for the officers doing the censoring either. One lieutenant described his first time censoring letters: "It is mighty hard for a boy to write home to his mother and tell her that his brother has been killed. I read two such letters in the first batch I censored. Each brother tried to tell how painless the death was, and how bravely the brother met it—but in each case I imagine the mother will think only of her loss, and not of the fact that her boy died a true American." Phelps Harding to C____, August 16, 1918, Imperial War Museum, London, J. Phelps Harding Collection, 1. For more on censorship, see Cooke, *Rainbow Division*, 84.

21. Both the Germans and the Allies used hydrogen gas balloons to observe their opponent's positions.

22. Cooke, *Rainbow Division*, 63.

23. Memorandum, February 17, 1918, in *United States Army in the World War*, vol. 2, 208.

24. Hugh S. Thompson, "Following the Rainbow," *Chattanooga Times*, January 14, 1934, Magazine Section, 1.

25. See H. A. Drum to Assistant Chief of Staff, March 27, 1918, in *United States Army in the World War*, vol. 3, 684; and Lt. Col. H. A. Drum to Col. Leroy Ettinge, March 14, 1918, ibid., 359.

26. See Memorandum to Chief Engineer, AEF, April 2, 1918, NA,

RG 120, World War I, Organizational Records, 42nd Division, Box 40–117th Engineers Regiment, Folder—117th Engineers History, 1; Memorandum to Chief Engineer, AEF, May 2, 1918, ibid., 1; Memorandum to Chief Engineer, AEF, June 5, 1918, ibid., 1; Memorandum to Chief Engineer, AEF, July 6, 1918, ibid., 1; and C.O., 117th Engineers Regiment to Commanding General, 42nd Division, April 9, 1918, ibid., Folder—117th Engineers Operational Memo. 1918 (April 11, 1918), 1–4.

27. Joseph Timmons, "117th Engineers, Heroes of Many Battles, Speed Westward," *Los Angeles Examiner*, May 11, 1919, UNLA, RDC, RDVA Papers, Oversize Folder 14, 5.

28. This average number of German shells fired was tabulated from the 42nd Division, Summary of Intelligence, February 21 to June 19, 1918. These reports can be found at UNLA, RDC, RDVA Papers, World War I. See also Reilly, *Americans All*, 123.

29. Frank T. Kolar, "So Far All In: Diary of a Common Soldier," UNLA, RDC, RDVA Papers, Individual Papers, Box 7, Folder 4, 40.

30. Quoted in Sadler, *California Rainbow Memories*, 27.

31. "Gas Alarm—Casualty Throws Ambulance Men," *Rainbow Reveille* 14, no. 3 (January–February 1935): 13. See also Cooke, *Rainbow Division*, 65–66.

32. 42nd Division, Daily Intelligence Report, March 6th to March 7th, 1918, UNLA, RDC, RDVA, World War, 2.

33. In the CR Rouge Bouquet Held by the 2nd Battalion of 165th A.I.R., March 7–8, 1918, NA, RG 120, World War I, Organizational Records, 42nd Division, Box 27, Folder—Rept. of Events in CR Rouge Bouquet, 1.

34. Cochrane, *42nd Division before Landres-et-St. Georges*, 83.

35. Parsons, *American Engineers*, 185–87.

36. Ettinger and Ettinger, *Doughboy with the Fighting Sixty-ninth*, 79. For a description of how mustard gas victims were treated, see "With the Rainbow Division in France," 10.

37. Summary of Intelligence, May 26 to May 27, 1918, UNLA, RDC, RDVA Papers, World War I, 1.

38. Taber, *Story of the 168th Infantry*, vol. 1, 222.

39. Taber, *Story of the 168th Infantry*, vol. 1, 225–26.

40. Reilly, *Americans All*, 207.

41. Reilly, *Americans All*, 198. See also "How We Went 'Over the Top,'" *Charleston News and Courier*, June 30, 1918, 5.

42. Wolf, *Brief History of the Rainbow Division*, 12, 19; and "How We Went 'Over the Top,'" *Charleston News and Courier*, June 30, 1918, 5. For what motivated soldiers to volunteer, see Kindsvatter, *American Soldiers*.

43. Other than this raid, the only over active missions were the patrols

sent out each day and night. See Summary of Intelligence, February 21 to June 19, 1918, UNLA, RDC, RDVA Papers, World War I.

44. Plan for Raid Upon the Bois des Chiens, April 8, 1918, NA, RG 120, 42nd Division, Box 9, Folder—42nd Division, G-3 Orders, 1.

45. "How We Went 'Over the Top,'" *Charleston News and Courier*, June 30, 1918, 5.

46. Reilly, *Americans All*, 198–99. See also Plan for Raid Upon the Bois des Chiens, April 8, 1918, NA, RG 120, World War I Organizational Records, 42nd Division, Box 9, Folder—42nd Division, G-3 Orders, 1.

47. Brigade Commander to Commanding General, 42nd Division, May 3, 1918, NA, RG 120, World War I, Organizational Records, 42nd Division, Box 13, Folder—42nd Division, Defense Scheme—Baccarat, 1.

48. Reilly, *Americans All*, 198–99.

49. C.O. 149th Field Artillery to Commanding General, 67th Field Artillery Brigade, May 5, 1918, USAMHI, Henry J. Reilly Papers, Box A, Folder—Coup de Main #4, 2.

50. "How We Went 'Over the Top,'" *Charleston News and Courier*, June 30, 1918, 5.

51. Summary of Intelligence, May 2 to May 3, 1918, UNLA, RDC, RDVA Papers, World War I, 2.

52. Tompkins, *Story of the Rainbow*, 38–39.

53. "How We Went 'Over the Top,'" *Charleston News and Courier*, June 30, 1918, 5.

54. Brigade Commander to Commanding General, 42nd Division, May 3, 1918, NA, RG 120, World War I, Organizational Records, 42nd Division, Box 13, Folder—42nd Division, Defense Scheme—Baccarat, 2.

55. Diary of Signal Platoon, Headquarters Co., 166th Infantry, 42nd Rainbow Division, UNLA, RDC, RDVA Papers, World War I, Box 2, Folder 7, 4.

56. Reilly, *Americans All*, 224–25.

4. Champagne and the Battle of Ourcq River

1. For descriptions of these battles, see Coffman, *War to End All Wars*, 156–58, 214–22.

2. Reilly, *Americans All*, 307.

3. American Battle Monuments Commission, *42nd Division*, 16, 32.

4. Brownie was near Saint-Germain.

5. Brownie was evidently staying near an artillery unit that was using a grove of trees for cover.

6. Dog tents were the tents used by the American soldiers. They could

be used individually to create a one-person tent or combined with one or three others to create either two- or four-person tents. The French 120s were artillery pieces.

7. Memorandum No. 212, June 24, 1918, NA, RG 120, World War I, Organizational Records, 42nd Division, Box 18, Folder—42nd Division, Training Memos and Programs 1918, 1.

8. See the Adjutant General to the Commanding General, 42nd Division, June 27, 1918, NA, RG 120, World War I, Organizational Records, 42nd Division, Box 18, Folder—42nd Division Training, 2; and Memorandum No. 218, June 30, 1918, ibid., Box 9, Folder—42nd Division G-3 Memos 1918, 2.

9. Memorandum from Pettelat, July 1, 1918, in *United States Army in the World War*, vol. 3, 714.

10. Pershing, *My Experiences*, vol. 2, 111.

11. Taber, *Story of the 168th Infantry*, vol. 1, 277.

12. MacArthur, *Reminiscences*, 57.

13. For a description of the elastic defense plan, see American Battle Monuments Commission, *42nd Division*, 13.

14. See Order of Battle, July 15, 1918, in *United States Army in the World War*, vol. 5, *Military Operations of the American Expeditionary Forces*, 2; General Order, July 15, 1918, NA, RG 120, World War I, Organizational Records, 42nd Division, Box 9, Folder—42nd Division Operation Orders (French), 1; and Cooke, *Rainbow Division*, 112.

15. Quoted in Sadler, *California Rainbow Memories*, 33.

16. General Hug, "The Battle of the 15th July 1918 on the Twentieth Anniversary, 1938," UNLA, RDC, RDVA Papers, Individual Papers, Box 8, Folder 1, 3.

17. U.S. Army, *Historical Report of the Chief Engineer*, 117.

18. Personal and Secret Instructions, July 3, 1918, NA, RG 120, World War I, Organizational Records, 42nd Division, Box 23, Folder—83rd Infantry Brigade, 1.

19. Memorandum No. 6, July 7, 1918, UNLA, RDC, RDVA Papers, RDVA Chapters, Box 5, Folder 12, 1.

20. Quoted in Sadler, *California Rainbow Memories*, 34.

21. George, *Challenge of War*, 68.

22. See Operations Report, French 4th Army, July 18, 1918, in *United States Army in the World War*, vol. 5, 152; and Summary of Events of July 15, 1918, NA, RG 120, World War I, Organizational Records, 42nd Division, Box 14, Folder—42nd Division, Summary of Events July 1918, 1.

23. Translations of Letters Found on the Two Prisoners, July 25, 1918, UNLA, RDC, RDVA, World War I Summaries of Intelligence, 1.

24. Quoted in Wolf, *Brief History of the Rainbow Division*, 25.

25. Duffy, *Father Duffy's Story*, 129–30.

26. *Americans Defending Democracy*, 62.

27. Diary of Erwin M. Johannes, USAMHI, World War I Military History Surveys, Box 42nd Division #3, 67th Field Artillery Brigade, Folder—WWI—6976, Johannes, Erwin M., 54.

28. Straub, *Sergeant's Diary*, 121.

29. Goode, *American Rainbow*, 7.

30. Quoted in Tompkins, *Story of the Rainbow Division*, 55.

31. John D. Brenner, "Le Guerre: 1917–1918-1919," UNLA, RDC, RDVA Papers, Individual Papers, Box 1, Folder 7, 20.

32. Stansbury, *Maryland's 117th Trench Mortar Battery*, 71.

33. Taber, *Story of the 168th Infantry*, vol. 1, 282.

34. Clarence W. Cox, "Private Clarence W. Cox, Headq. Co., 167th Infantry Relates His Most Exciting Experience," *Army and Navy Record, April 1920,* 32.

35. Evans, *American Voices*, 91.

36. "Francois 570," *Rainbow Reveille* (June-July 1927): 3.

37. Maj. James A. Frew, "Experiences with the Rainbow Division," UNLA, RDC, RDVA Papers, World War I, Box 2, Folder 14, 8–9.

38. Sgt. Tom Witworth to L. R. Allison, August 22, 1918, USAMHI, Henry J. Reilly Papers, Box 83, Folder—Chapter 14, Champagne, 2.

39. Summary of Events of July 15, 1918, NA, RG 120, World War I, Organizational Records, 42nd Division, Box 14, Folder—42nd Division, Summary of Events July 1918, 1.

40. Summary of Events of July 16, 1918, NA, RG 120, World War I, Organizational Records, 42nd Division, Box 14, Folder—42nd Division, Summary of Events July 1918, 1.

41. Bulletin of Information No. 5, July 17, 1918, UNLA, RDC, RDVA, World War I, Summaries of Intelligence, 1.

42. General Naulin to French 4th Army, 21st Army Corps, July 15, 1918, UNLA, RDC, RDVA, World War I, Box 1, Folder 10, 1.

43. War Diary of W. G. Hudson, 1917–1918, Connecticut Historical Society, Hartford CT, 33.

44. Historical Notes, 167th U.S. Infantry, Battle of Champagne, July 15, 1918, USAMHI, Henry J. Reilly Papers, Box 43, 15.

45. American Battle Monuments Commission, *42nd Division*, 16.

46. *Americans Defending Democracy*, 67.

47. War Diary of W. G. Hudson, 1917–1918, Connecticut Historical Society, Hartford CT, 38.

48. Quoted in Farwell, *Over There: United States*, 180.

49. Sadler, *California Rainbow Memories*, 40.

50. Quoted in Farwell, *Over There: United States*, 111.

51. Sgt. Tom Witworth to L. R. Allison, August 22, 1918, USAMHI, Henry J. Reilly Papers, Box 83, Folder—Chapter 14, Champagne, 2.

52. General Orders No. 48, July 20, 1918, UNLA, RDC, RDVA Papers, World War I, Box 1, Folder 9, 1.

53. Stallings, *Doughboys: Story*, 138.

54. French Military Mission, American 42nd Division, July 17, 1918, in *United States Army in the World War*, vol. 5, 171.

55. See *United States Army in the World War*, vol. 1, 27; Johnson and Hillman, *Soissons*, 35–36; Bridges, "Through the Fire," 71; and Special Orders No. 3543, July 21, 1918, in *United States Army in the World War*, vol. 5, 171.

56. See Cooke, *Rainbow Division*, 118–20; Wolf, *Brief History of the Rainbow*, 33–34; and Memorandum for the American I Army Corps, July 23, 1918, in *United States Army in the World War*, vol. 5, 365.

57. Brown, "In Action with the Rainbow Division," 38.

58. Evans, *American Voices*, 108.

59. Quoted in Hallas, *Doughboy War*, 124.

60. Quoted in Collins, *Minnesota in the War*, 86.

61. Sherwood, *Diary of a Rainbow Veteran*, 35.

62. Straub, *Sergeant's Diary*, 133.

63. Transcript of Medical Detachment of the 117th Engineers, UNLA, RDC, RDVA Papers, World War I, Box 2, Folder 5, 12.

64. Stallings, *Doughboys: Story*, 162.

65. Diary of Norman L. Summers, USAMHI, Henry J. Reilly Papers, 42nd Division, Box 42nd Division, 84th Infantry Brigade, Folder—WWI—3477, Summers, Norman L.

66. Baker, *Doughboy's Diary*, 70.

67. Ettinger and Ettinger, *A Doughboy with the Fighting Sixty-ninth*, 130.

68. Edmund F. Hackett, "The Fight at Croix Rouge Farm," *Army and Navy Record*, April 1920, 30.

69. Lieutenant Lurte [?], Chapter 8—Alabama's First Attack, USAMHI, Henry J. Reilly Papers, Box 43, 12–13.

70. "Other Gripping Narratives of the Old Fourth's Action at the Battle of Croix Rouge Farm," *Army and Navy Record*, April 1920, 40.

71. Amerine, *Alabama's Own*, 150.

72. Operations Report, 42nd Division, American E.F., July 25–August 3, 1918, NA, RG 120, World War I, Organizational Records, 42nd Division, Box 14, Folder—42nd Div. Ops. Rept. July 25–Aug. 3, 1918, 1.

73. Reilly, *Americans All*, 346.

74. Ettinger and Ettinger, *Doughboy with the Fighting Sixty-ninth*, 130.

75. Sherwood, *Diary of a Rainbow Veteran*, 40.

76. Diary of Norman L. Summers, USAMHI, Henry J. Reilly Papers,

Box 42nd Division, 84th Infantry Brigade, Folder—WWI—3477, Summers, Norman L.

77. Quoted in Hallas, *Doughboy Wars*, 164.

78. Summary of Intelligence, July 27 to July 18, 1918, UNLA, RDC, RDVA, World War I, Summaries of Intelligence, 2. See also Field Orders No. 27, July 27, 1918, NA, RG 120, World War I, Organizational Records, 42nd Division, Box 8, Folder—42nd Field Orders re 42nd Division, 1.

79. Taber, *Story of the 168th Infantry*, vol. 1, 352.

80. Summary of Intelligence, July 27 to July 28, 1918, UNLA, RDC, RDVA, World War I, Summaries of Intelligence, 1.

81. See Information about the Ourcq in Our Sector, July 26, 1918, UNLA, RDC, RDVA, World War I, Box 1, Folder 9, 1; Tompkins, *Story of the Rainbow Division*, 80; and "Rainbow Division Hurls Boche Back From Ourcq Line," *Stars and Stripes*, January 24, 1919, 8; and "Yankees Humble Germany's Best in Ourcq Battle," *Stars and Stripes*, August 2, 1918, 2.

82. See Information about the Ourcq in Our Sector, July 26, 1918, UNLA, RDC, RDVA, World War I, Box 1, Folder 9, 1; Tompkins, *Story of the Rainbow Division*, 80; "Rainbow Division Hurls Boche Back From Ourcq Line," *Stars and Stripes*, January 24, 1919, 8; and "Col. Johnson and Engineers Arrive," *Charleston News and Courier*, April 29, 1919, 4.

83. "Engineers' Task Not Ended When Vesle is Spanned," *Stars and Stripes*, August 16, 1918, 5.

84. "Review of Work of Engineers; a True Story about Our Fighters," *Marion Star*, May 14, 1919, 1.

85. Field Orders No. 27, July 27, 1918, NA, RG 120, World War I, Organizational Records, 42nd Division, Box 8, Folder—42nd Field Orders re 42nd Division, 1.

86. Field Orders No. 26, July 27, 1918, NA, RG 120, World War I, Organizational Records, 42nd Division, Box 8, Folder—42nd Field Orders re 42nd Division, 1.

87. Information about the Ourcq in Our Sector, July 26, 1918, UNLA, RDC, RDVA Papers, World War I, Box 1, Folder 9, 1.

88. Field Orders No. 26, July 27, 1918, NA, RG 120, World War I, Organizational Records, 42nd Division, Box 8, Folder—42nd Field Orders re 42nd Division, 2. See also General Orders No. 51, July 27, 1918, UNLA, RDC, RDVA Papers, World War I, Box 1, Folder 9, 1.

89. Summary of Intelligence, No. 25, July 29, 1918, in *United States Army in the World War*, vol. 5, 458.

90. Letter from Lt. Alexandre Winter in William Donovan's Letters from France, USAMHI, Henry J. Reilly Papers, 42nd Division, Box—Diaries and Reports from 1910 to 1919, 106.

91. Quoted in Collins, *Minnesota in the War*, 99.

92. Personal Experiences, Observations, and Incidents Compiled from Notes, Orders, Messages and Memory of Isaac G. Walker, Former First Lieutenant Company A, 151st Machine Gun Battalion, 42nd Division, USAMHI, World War I Military History Surveys, 42nd Division, 84th Infantry Brigade, Folder—Isaac G. Walker, Co. A, 151st Machine Gun Battalion, World War I Survey, 6.

93. Taber, *Story of the 168th Infantry*, vol. 1, 373–74.

94. Testimony of Maj. William J. Donovan, 165th Infantry, August 15, 1918, NA, RG 120, World War I, Organizational Records, 42nd Division, Box 27, Folder—165th Inf. Rept. of Maj. Wm. Donovan, Aug. 15/18, 1.

95. Report on Experiences as Infantry Liaison Officer during the Fighting, August 20, 1918, USAMHI, Henry J. Reilly Papers, World War I, Box E, Folder 5–9-23 Sept, 5.

96. Summary of Intelligence, July 28 to July 29, 1918, UNLA,RDC, RDVA, World War I, Summaries of Intelligence, 1.

97. MacArthur, *Reminiscences*, 59.

98. Summary of Intelligence, No. 28, August 1, 1918, in *United States Army in the World War*, vol. 5, 467.

99. Summary of Intelligence, July 29 to July 30, 1918, UNLA, RDC, RDVA, World War I, Summaries of Intelligence, 1.

100. Taber, *Story of the 168th Infantry*, vol. 2, 9.

101. Field Orders No. 32, July 31, 1918, NA, RG 120, World War I, Organizational Records, 42nd Division, Box 8, Folder—42nd Field Orders re 42nd Division, 1.

102. See Summary of Intelligence, July 31 to August 1, 1918, UNLA, RDC, RDVA, World War I, Summaries of Intelligence, 2; and Summary of Intelligence, August 1 to August 2, 1918, ibid., 1; Memorandum, August 1, 1918, in *United States Army in the World War*, vol. 5, 527; and Cooke, *Rainbow Division*, 131–32.

103. Reilly, *Americans All*, 343.

104. "S.C. Boys on the Heels of the Huns," *Charleston News and Courier*, September 22, 1918, 8.

105. Summary of Intelligence, No. 118, August 1–2, 1918 in *United States Army in the World War*, vol. 5, 528.

106. See Commanding General, Army Corps, A.E.F. to Commanding General, 6th Army, August 28, 1918 in *United States Army in the World War*, vol. 5, 456; Operations Report, 42nd Division, American E.F., July 25–August 3, 1918, NA, RG 120, World War I, Organizational Records, 42nd Division, Box 14, Folder—42nd Div. Ops. Rept. July 25–Aug. 3, 1918, 2; and Reilly, *Americans All*, 480.

107. American Battle Monuments Commission, *42nd Division*, 33.

108. "River Ourcq Runs Red with Blood Where Americans Triumph Over Prussian Guard," *Charleston News and Courier*, July 30, 1918, 1.

109. "Yankees Humble Germany's Best in Ourcq Battle," *Stars and Stripes*, August 2, 1918, 1.

110. John D. Brenner, "Le Guerre: 1917–1918-1919," UNLA, RDC, RDVA Papers, Individual Papers, Box 1, Folder 7, 27.

111. Horry Hunter, Army Service Questionnaire, USAMHI, World War I Military History Surveys, Box 42nd Rainbow Division #2, 83rd Infantry Brigade, Folder—WWI—3589, Hunter, Harry, 11.

112. Straub, *A Soldier's Diary*, 144–5.

113. John D. Brenner, "Le Guerre: 1917–1918-1919," UNLA, RDC, RDVA Papers, Individual Papers, Box 1, Folder 7, 34.

114. Ibid., 43.

115. Memorandum to Chief Engineer, AEF, October 6, 1918, NA, RG 120, World War I, Organizational Records, 42nd Division, Box 40–117th Engineers Regiment, Folder—117th Engineers History, 1. Until August, American units fought in conjunction with French and British armies. In August 1918 the First American Army was created. See Coffman, *War to End All Wars*, 262–64.

5. Rest and the Battle of Saint-Mihiel

1. Memorandum to Chief Engineer, AEF, October 6, 1918, NA, RG 120, World War I, Organizational Records, 42nd Division, Box 40–117th Engineers Regiment, Folder—117th Engineers History, 1. A salient is a protrusion of territory in front of a relatively straight defensive position.

2. Amerine, *Alabama's Own*, 164.

3. Reilly, *Americans All*, 514.

4. Janis was a twenty-nine-year-old singer and dancer who traveled around France entertaining the American soldiers. See Phelps Harding to C____, August 16, 1918, Imperial War Museum, London, J. Phelps Harding Collection, 1; Freidel, *Over There: Story*, 194; and "Elsie One of Us While War Lasts," *Stars and Stripes*, March 29, 1918, 7.

5. Cooke, *Rainbow Division*, 140–43. See also Phelps Harding to C____, August 16, 1918, Imperial War Museum, London, J. Phelps Harding Collection, 2.

6. See Corey, "Cooties and Courage," 409–509; and Phelps Harding to Mother, July 5, 1918, Imperial War Museum, London, J. Phelps Harding Collection, 1.

7. Sherwood, *Diary of a Rainbow Veteran*, 68.

8. Phelps Harding to Mother, July 5, 1918, Imperial War Museum, London, J. Phelps Harding Collection, 1–2.

9. Taber, *Story of the 168th Infantry*, vol. 2, 58.

10. Nenninger, "Tactical Dysfunction," 178.

11. See *United States Army in the World War*, vol. 1, 142–43.

12. Gilbert, *First World War: A Complete History*, 85.

13. Memorandum for GHQ, February 18, 1918, in *United States Army in the World War*, vol. 2, 210–14.

14. See Memorandum to Chief of Staff, First Army, and August 16, 1918, in *United States Army in the World War*, vol. 8, *Military Operations of American Expeditionary Forces*, 130; Braim, *Test of Battle*, 77; and Trask, AEF *and Coalition Warmaking*, 106.

15. It was not unusual for engineers to precede infantry in attacks to clear and/or mark paths through the wire for the advancing soldiers.

16. See *Order of Battle*, vol. 2, 276–86; Reilly, *Americans All*, 532; and Cooke, *Rainbow Division*, 149.

17. See Wolf, *Brief Story of the Rainbow*, 37; and Hallas, *Squandered Victory*, 65.

18. Quoted in Hallas, *Squandered Victory*, 6.

19. Narrative of Leland L. Whitney, 166th Infantry Regiment Concerning World War I Service, UNLA, RDC, RDVA, Individual Papers, Box 8, Folder 1, 25. See also Hallas, *Doughboy War*, 224, 228.

20. Diary of Signal Platoon, Headquarters Co., 166th Infantry, 42nd Rainbow Division, UNLA, RDC, RDVA Papers, World War I, Box 2, Folder 7, 9.

21. Duffy, *Father Duffy's Story*, 234.

22. These quotes come from captured German letters that were translated and included in Summary of Intelligence, September 18, 1918, UNLA, RDC, RDVA, World War I, Summaries of Intelligence, 1–2.

23. See Tompkins, *Story of the Rainbow Division*, 117; and "Review of Work of Engineers; a True Story about Our Fighters," *Marion Star*, May 14, 1919, 1.

24. See American Battle Monuments Commission, *42nd Division*, 40; and Addendum No. 1 to Field Order No. 17 and Annex No. 2—Plan for the Employment of Engineers, September 11, 1918, USAMHI, Henry J. Reilly Papers, 42nd Division, Box—Letters and Reports Re: WW 1, 42nd Division, 1–2.

25. "History of the 117th Engineers Story of Training and Fighting," *Marion Star*, March 12, 1919, 1.

26. Field Order No. 17, September 9, 1918, USAMHI, Henry J. Reilly Papers, Box—Letters and Reports Re: WW 1, 42nd Division, 2.

27. Duffy, *Father Duffy's Story*, 235.

28. Sherwood, *Diary of a Rainbow Veteran*, 105.

29. See Summary of Intelligence, September 11 to September 12, 1918, UNLA, RDC, RDVA, World War I Summaries of Intelligence, 1; and Farwell, *Over There: United States*, 212.

30. Harding to Christine, September 22, 1918, in Clark and Clark, "New York Yank Narrates a Costly Victory," 5.

31. Lawrence, *Fighting Soldier*, 61.

32. Capt. [?], St. Mihiel No. 10, USAMHI, Henry J. Reilly Papers, Box 43, 10.

33. Taber, *Story of the 168th Infantry*, vol. 2, 85.

34. Quoted in Hallas, *Doughboy War*, 228.

35. Capt. [?], St. Mihiel #10, USAMHI, Henry J. Reilly Papers, Box 43, 10.

36. See Farwell, *Over There: United States*, 213; and Cooke, *Rainbow Division*, 147–48.

37. Some Recollections of the St. Mihiel Attack by a Platoon Leader, Lt. R. R. DeLacour, USAMHI, Henry J. Reilly Papers, Box 83, Folder— Chapter 20, Battle of St. Mihiel, 1.

38. Taber, *Story of the 168th Infantry*, vol. 2, 92.

39. Tompkins, *Story of the Rainbow Division*, 112.

40. Quoted in Hallas, *Doughboy War*, 226.

41. See Hallas, *Squandered Victory*, 28–29, 77, 82; Summary of Intelligence, September 11 to September 12, 1918, UNLA, RDC, RDVA, World War I, Summaries of Intelligence, 1; Summary of Intelligence, September 12 to September 13, 1918, ibid., 1; and Summary of Intelligence, September 13 to September 14, 1918, ibid., 1.

42. Taber, *Story of the 168th Infantry*, vol. 2., 99.

43. Summary of Intelligence, September 12 to September 13, 1918, UNLA, RDC, RDVA, World War I, Summaries of Intelligence, 1.

44. Summary of Intelligence, September 11 to September 12, 1918, UNLA, RDC, RDVA, World War I, Summaries of Intelligence, 2.

45. See Summary of Intelligence, September 12 to September 13, 1918, UNLA, RDC, RDVA, World War I, Summaries of Intelligence, 2; Summary of Intelligence, September 13 to September 14, 1918, ibid., 1; Summary of Intelligence, September 14 to September 15, 1918, ibid., 1; Summary of Intelligence, September 15 to September 16, 1918, ibid., 1; and Tompkins, *Story of the Rainbow Division*, 115–16.

46. Special Note on German Opinion of American Troops, no date, UNLA, RDC, RDVA, World War I, Summaries of Intelligence, 1. See also Headquarters 42nd Division, September 16, 1918, ibid., 2; and Report of Interrogation of 5 German Prisoners, September 17, 1918, ibid., 1.

47. Harding to Christine, September 22, 1918, in Clark and Clark, "New York Yank Narrates a Costly Victory," 5.

48. Harding to Christine, September 22, 1918, in Clark and Clark, "New York Yank Narrates a Costly Victory," 5.

49. Quoted in Hallas, *Doughboy War*, 233.

50. Joseph, *WW I Diary of Pvt. Emile M. Calhoun*, 61, 63.

51. American Battle Monuments Commission, *42nd Division*, 50.

52. The sneezing gas was probably derived from diphenylchlorarsine. World War I soldiers nicknamed it "blue cross."

53. See Memorandum to Chief Engineer, AEF, October 6, 1918, NA, RG 120, World War I, Organizational Records, 42nd Division, Box 40–117th Engineers Regiment, Folder—117th Engineers History, 1; and Diary of Signal Platoon, Headquarters Co., 166th Infantry, 42nd Rainbow Division, UNLA, RDC, RDVA Papers, World War I, Box 2, Folder 7, 10.

54. See Summary of Intelligence, September 25 to September 26, 1918, UNLA, RDC, RDVA, World War I, Summaries of Intelligence, 2; MacArthur, *Reminiscences*, 64; and Cooke, *Rainbow Division*, 158–59.

55. Brownie is referring to the artillery barrage that marked the beginning of the last great German offensive in Champagne the night of July 14–15.

56. Phelps Harding to Mother, October 8, 1918, Imperial War Museum, London, J. Phelps Harding Collection, 1.

6. The End of the War

1. Coffman, *War to End All Wars*, 299–304.

2. Gilbert, *First World War: A Complete History*, 465–67.

3. See Braim, *Test of Battle*, 74; and Farwell, *Over There: United States*, 218.

4. Taber, *Story of the 165th Infantry*, vol. 2, 160.

5. Roth and Wheeler, *History of Company "E"*, 123.

6. See Stallings, *Doughboys: Story*, 229.

7. Final Report of Gen. John J. Pershing, September 1, 1919, UNLA, RDC, World War I, Box 2, Folder 1, 20.

8. Braim, *Test of Battle*, 58, 96. While he could do little about it, Pershing did recognize the problem of inadequate training as early as April 1918. See For the Chief of Staff and Secretary of War, April 24, 1918, in *United States Army in the World War*, vol. 2, 344.

9. "Gas Alarm—Landres-St. Georges," *Rainbow Reveille* 14, no. 4 (May–June 1935): 14.

10. See Braim, *Test of Battle*, 79; and Farwell, *Over There: United States*, 222.

11. Phelps Harding to Mother, October 8, 1918, Imperial War Museum, London, J. Phelps Harding Collection, 1.

12. Braim, *Test of Battle*, 82.

13. Triplet, *A Youth in the Meuse-Argonne*, 196.

14. Baker, *Doughboy's Diary*, 99.

15. Triplet, *A Youth in the Meuse-Argonne*, 171.

16. Triplet, *A Youth in the Meuse-Argonne*, 173. Out of Triplet's platoon of fifty-one, only seven escaped being killed or wounded. See ibid., 249.

17. Braim, *Test of Battle*, 112.

18. Quoted in Hallas, *Doughboy War*, 153.

19. Quoted in Hallas, *Doughboy War*, 248.

20. G-3 Special Orders No. 314, September 29, 1918, in *United States Army in the World War*, vol. 9, *Military Operations of the American Expeditionary Forces*, 154.

21. Sherwood, *Diary of a Rainbow Veteran*, 161.

22. Quoted in Cooke, *Rainbow Division*, 166.

23. Field Orders No. 35, October 2, 1918, in *United States Army in the World War*, vol. 9, 195.

24. Memorandum to Chief Engineer, AEF, November 6, 1918, NA, RG 120, World War I, Organizational Records, 42nd Division, Box 40–117th Engineers Regiment, Folder—117th Engineers History, 1–2.

25. Brown, "In Action with the Rainbow Division," 38.

26. Quoted in Collins, *Minnesota in the World War*, 141–42.

27. Ettinger and Ettinger, *Doughboy with the Fighting Sixty-ninth*, 156.

28. See Summary of Intelligence, October 12–13, 1918, UNLA, RDC, RDVA, World War I, Summary of Intelligence, 1; and Summary of Intelligence, October 12, 1918, ibid., 1.

29. Taber, *Story of the 168th Infantry*, vol. 2, 168.

30. Duffy, *Father Duffy's Story*, 265. See also Stallings, *Doughboys: Story*, 333.

31. Reilly, *Americans All*, 642.

32. Collins, *Minnesota in the World War*, 146.

33. Summary of Intelligence, October 13–14, 1918, UNLA, RDC, RDVA, World War I, Summaries of Intelligence, 2.

34. C-201, October 15, 1918, in *United States Army in the World War*, vol. 9, 275. See also OP/13, October 16, 1918, in ibid., 281.

35. Summary of Intelligence, October 13–14, 1918, UNLA, RDC, RDVA, World War I, Summaries of Intelligence, 1.

36. Phelps Harding to Mother, October 25, 1918, Imperial War Museum, London, J. Phelps Harding Collection, 1.

37. Summary of Intelligence, October 13–14, 1918, UNLA, RDC, RDVA, World War I, Summaries of Intelligence, 1.

38. Phelps Harding to Mother, October 25, 1918, Imperial War Museum, London, J. Phelps Harding Collection, 1.

39. I. G. Walker, "Remember Armistice Day Formations?," *Rainbow Reveille* 44, no. 3 (November 1965), 3.

40. Ettinger and Ettinger, *Doughboy with the Fighting Sixty-ninth*, 162.

41. Summary of Intelligence, October 14–15, 1918, UNLA, RDC, RDVA,

World War I, Summaries of Intelligence, 1–2. See also OP/13, October 16, 1918, in *United States Army in the World War*, vol. 9, 195.

42. See Summary of Intelligence, October 16–17, 1918, UNLA, RDC, RDVA, World War I, Summaries of Intelligence, 2; and Summary of Intelligence, October 15–16, 1918, ibid., 2.

43. Summary of Intelligence, October 15–16, 1918, UNLA, RDC, RDVA, World War I, Summaries of Intelligence, 1.

44. Memo to Chief Engineer, AEF, November 6, 1918, NA, RG 120, World War I, Organizational Records, 42nd Division, Box 40–117th Engineers Regiment, Folder, 117th Engineers History, 1.

45. Cooke, *Rainbow Division*, 176.

46. Ettinger and Ettinger, *Doughboy with the Fighting Sixty-ninth*, 161.

47. See Reilly, *Americans All*, 663.

48. Report of the First Army, the Second Operation, in *United States Army in the World War*, vol. 9, 366.

49. Summary of Intelligence, October 17–18, 1918, UNLA, RDC, RDVA, World War I, Summaries of Intelligence, 1.

50. Summary of Intelligence, October 18–19, 1918, UNLA, RDC, RDVA, World War I, Summaries of Intelligence, 1.

51. See Summary of Intelligence, October 19–20, 1918, UNLA, RDC, RDVA, World War I, Summaries of Intelligence, 1; Summary of Intelligence, October 19–20, 1918, ibid., 1; Summary of Intelligence, October 22–23, 1918, ibid., 1; Summary of Intelligence, October 23–24, 1918, ibid., 1; Summary of Intelligence, October 26–27, 1918, ibid., 1; Summary of Intelligence, October 27–28, 1918, ibid., 1; and Summary of Intelligence, October 30–31, 1918, ibid., 1.

52. Cooke, *Rainbow Division*, 187.

53. "With the Rainbow Division in France," 12.

54. Phelps Harding to Mother, October 8, 1918, Imperial War Museum, London, J. Phelps Harding Collection, 1.

55. Baker, *Doughboy's Diary*, 93.

56. Joseph, *WW I Diary of Pvt. Emile M. Calhoun*, 87.

57. Duffy, *Father Duffy's Story*, 290.

58. Stansbury, *Maryland's 117th Trench Mortar Battery*, 102.

59. Triplet, *A Youth in the Meuse-Argonne*, 260.

60. Joseph, *WW I Diary of Pvt. Emile M. Calhoun*, 89. For other descriptions of casualties, see Lawrence, *Fighting Soldier*, 81.

61. "Brest Worse than the Front," *Waterbury Republican*, March 2, 1919, 9.

62. Brownie mentioned in his October 30 letter to Marty that he had been at the hospital for a week; therefore, he had to have been gassed sometime in the last weeks of October. The Germans launched 200 gas shells the night on October 21–22, 100 on October 22–23,

and 230 on October 23–24. See Summary of Intelligence, October 21–22, 1918, UNLA, RDC, RDVA, World War I, Summaries of Intelligence, 1; Summary of Intelligence, October 22–23, 1918, ibid., 1; Summary of Intelligence, October 23–24, 1918, ibid., 1; and Honorable Discharge of George Browne, Army of the United States, February 18, 1919, in author's possession.

63. Summary of Intelligence, October 27–28, 1918, UNLA, RDC, RDVA, World War I, Summaries of Intelligence, 1.

64. Frank T. Kolar, "So Far All In: Diary of a Common Soldier," UNLA, RDC, RDVA Papers, Individual Papers, Box 7, Folder 4, 108.

65. "With the Rainbow Division in France," 10.

66. "From Somewhere on the Other Side," *Charleston News and Courier*, October 6, 1918, 18.

67. Cochrane, *Use of Gas in the Meuse-Argonne Campaign*, 77–79.

68. He is referring to the battle of the Meuse-Argonne.

69. See G-3, No. 29, November 11, 1918, in *United States Army in the World War*, vol. 9, 371; G-3, No. 30, November 12, 1918, in ibid., 376; No. 34, November 6, 1918, in ibid., 389; 3rd Section, November 10, 1918, in ibid., 409; Summary of Intelligence, November 6–7, 1918, UNLA, RDC, RDVA, World War I, Summaries of Intelligence, 1–2; Braim, *Test of Battle*, 103, 137, and Cooke, *Rainbow Division*, 163.

70. Keegan, *First World War*, 423.

71. Casualty figures for all American wars, including World War I, can be found at the Department of Defense Web site, http://web1.whs.osd .mil/mmid/m01/SMS223R.HTM. See also Stallings, *Doughboys: Story*, 380.

Conclusion

1. "Can" was slang for the guardhouse.

2. Brownie's platoon preceded the infantry either in the Aisne-Marne offensive in July or in the Argonne Forest in October.

3. Stallings, *Doughboys: Story*, 184.

4. Marty is referring to Brownie's letter from October 30, 1918 (see chapter 6). Brownie mentioned having been sick and in the hospital but provided no other details.

5. Martha Johnson to George Browne, November 27, 1918, in author's possession.

6. Cooke, *Rainbow Division*, 202, 214, 220–21.

7. See Coffman, *War to End All Wars*, 358–59; and Cooke, *Rainbow Division*, 212–24, 221–25.

8. See Cooke, *Rainbow Division*, 239; "Johnson Engineers Landed in New York Late Monday," *Marion Star*, April 30, 1918, 1; Bond and

Sherrill, *America in the World War*, 56–57; and Eisenhower, *Yanks*, 288.

9. See Farwell, *Over There: United States*, 58; Braim, *Test of Battle*, 150; Bond and Sherrill, *America in the World War*, 102, 109; and "Johnson's Men Work and Fight," *The State*, April 29, 1919, 1.

10. Honorable Discharge of George Browne, Army of the United States, February 18, 1919, in author's possession.

11. "Wolcott," *Waterbury Republican*, August 14, 1919, 13.

12. They did not always reside in Waterbury, as Brownie's engineering work sometimes required him to work on projects some distance from the city that were related to transporting water from the Shepaug River by tunnels to the Waterbury reservoir.

13. One of Brownie's major assignments was to help construct a tunnel connecting Bantam Lake to a reservoir for Waterbury. The tunnel went under part of the town of Morris. See Sando Bologna, "Water for Waterbury through . . . The Shepaug Connection," October 24, 1976, Morris Historical Society, Morris CT, 3–6.

14. Janet Hansen to author, July 1, 2003, in author's possession. Brownie and Marty's relatives remember stories about the couple's inability to have children possibly because of Brownie's injuries during the war.

Primary Sources

Personal Collections in Author's Possession

Letters from George Browne to Martha Johnson
Letters from Martha Johnson to George Browne
Miscellaneous Letters to George Browne

Archives and Historical Societies

Connecticut Historical Society (Hartford CT)
Connecticut State Library and Archives (Hartford CT)
Imperial War Museum (London)
   J. Phelps Harding Collection
MacArthur Memorial Library and Archives (Norfolk VA)
   Cleon Stanley Collection
   Harry Kendall Collection
   Homer Gardner Collection
   Townshend Collection
   William Severe Collection
Morris Historical Society (Morris CT)
National Archives of the United States (College Park MD)
   Record Group 120—Records of the American Expeditionary Forces
     (World War I)
U.S. Army Military History Institute (Carlisle Barracks PA)
   42nd Division Collection
   Henry J. Reilly Papers
   World War I Military History Surveys
U.S. Military Academy Special Collections (West Point)
   Charles Menoher Papers
University of Nebraska–Lincoln Love Library (Lincoln NE)
   Rainbow Division Collection

Government Publications

American Battle Monuments Commission. *American Armies and Battle-fields in Europe: A History, Guide, and Reference Book.* Washington DC: United States Government Printing Office, 1938.

————. *42nd Division: Summary of Operations in the World War.* Washington DC: United States Government Printing Office, 1944.

Battle Participation of Organizations of the American Expeditionary Forces in France, Belgium and Italy, 1917–1918. Washington DC: United States Government Printing Office, 1920.

Bayne-Jones, Stanhope. *The Evolution of Preventive Medicine in the United States Army.* Washington DC: Office of the Surgeon General, Department of the Army, 1968.

Cochrane, Rexmond C. *The Use of Gas in the Meuse-Argonne Campaign, September–November 1918.* Gas Warfare in World War I, Study Number 10. Army Chemical Center MD: U.S. Army Chemical Corps Historical Office, Office of the Chief Chemical Officer, 1958.

————. *The 42nd Division before Landres-et-St. Georges.* Army Chemical Center MD: U.S. Army Chemical Corps History Office, 1959.

Hamburger, Kenneth E. *Learning Lessons in the American Expeditionary Forces.* Washington DC: U.S. Army, Center of Military History, 1997.

Hendricks, Charles. *Combat and Construction: U.S. Army Engineers in World War I.* Fort Belvoir VA: Office of History, U.S. Army Corps of Engineers, 1993.

Kreidberg, Marvin A., and Merton G. Henry. *History of Military Mobilization in the United States Army, 1775–1945.* Washington DC: Department of the Army, 1955.

Monographs of the World War. Ft. Benning GA: U.S. Infantry School, 1923.

Order of Battle of the United States Land Forces in the World War. Vol. 2, *American Expeditionary Forces: Divisions.* Washington DC: Center of Military History, U.S. Army, 1988.

————. Vol. 3, *Zone of the Interior,* pt. 2, *Territorial Departments, Tactical Divisions Organized in 1918 Posts, Camps, and Stations.* Washington DC: Center of Military History, United States Army, 1988.

Service Records: Connecticut Men and Women in the Armed Forces of the United States During World War, 1917–1920. Office of the Adjutant General State Armory, Hartford CT. New Haven CT: United Printing Services, 1933.

Siler, Joseph F. *The Medical Department of the United States Army in the World War.* Vol. 9. *Communicable and Other Diseases.* Washington DC: U.S. Government Printing Office, 1928.

United States Army in the World War, 1917–1919. Vols. 1–17. Washington DC: Center of Military History, U.S. Army, 1988–92.

U.S. Army, American Expeditionary Forces, 1917–1920, Engineer Department. *Historical Report of the Chief Engineer, Including All Operations of the Engineer Department, American Expeditionary Forces, 1917–1919.* Washington DC: United States Government Printing Office, 1919.

U.S. Army, First Army, Engineer Section. *Report of the Chief Engineer, First Army, American Expeditionary Forces on the Engineer Operations in the St. Mihiel and Meuse-Argonne Offensives, 1918.* Occasional Papers No. 69, the Engineer School, U.S. Army. Washington DC: U.S. Government Printing Office, 1929.

U.S. Bureau of the Census. The Statistical History of the United States: From Colonial Times to the Present. New York: Basic Books, 1976.

Articles, Books, Diaries, and Memoirs

Americans Defending Democracy: Our Soldiers' Own Stories. New York: World's War Stories, 1919.

Amerine, William H. *Alabama's Own in France.* New York: Eaton & Gettinger, 1919.

The Army and Navy Record, April 1920, 1–95.

Baker, C. Earl. *Doughboy's Diary.* Shippensburg PA: Burd Street Press, 1998.

Brown, J. Douglas. "In Action with the Rainbow Division, 1918–19," *Military Review* 58, no. 1 (January 1978): 38–41.

Clark, George B., ed. *His Time in Hell: A Texas Marine in France, the Memoir of Warren R. Jackson.* Novato CA: Presidio Press, 2001.

Duffy, Francis P. *Father Duffy's Story: A Tale of Humor and Heroism, of Life and Death with the Fighting Sixty-ninth.* New York: George H. Doran, 1919.

Ettinger, Albert M., and A. Churchill Ettinger. *A Doughboy with the Fighting Sixty-ninth: A Remembrance of World War I.* Shippensburg PA: White Mane, 1992.

Evans, Martin Marix, ed. *American Voices of World War I: Primary Source Documents, 1917–1920.* London: Fitzroy Dearborn, 2001.

George, Herbert. *The Challenge of War.* New York: Vantage, 1966.

Harbord, James G. *The American Army in France, 1917–1919.* Boston MA: Little, Brown, 1936.

Haswell, William S., and Charles S. Stevenson. *A History of Company A-314th Engineers, 89th Division.* 1921.

Hurley, Edward N. *The Bridge to France.* Philadelphia PA: J. B. Lippincott, 1927.

Johnson, Harold Stanley, ed. *Roster of the Rainbow Division (Forty-Second), Major-General Wm. A. Mann Commanding.* New York: Eaton & Gettinger, 1917.

Joseph, Michael C. *WW I Diary of Pvt. Emile M. Calhoun, April 1918–June 1919: 353rd Infantry Medical Detachment 89th Division.* Independence MO: Two Trails Publishing, 1999.

Lawrence, Joseph Douglas. *Fighting Soldier: The AEF in 1918.* Boulder: Colorado Associated University Press, 1985.

MacArthur, Douglas. *Reminiscences.* New York: McGraw-Hill, 1964.

Mayo, Katherine. *"That Damn Y": A Record of Overseas Service.* Boston: Houghton Mifflin, 1920.

McCormick, Robert R. *The Army of 1918.* New York: Harcourt, Brace & Howe, 1920.

Parsons, William Barclay. *The American Engineers in France.* New York: D. Appleton, 1920.

Pershing, John J. *My Experiences in the World War.* 2 vols. New York: Frederick A. Stokes, 1931.

Roth, Joseph P., and Robert L. Wheeler. *History of Company "E" 303rd Engineers of the 78th Division, 1917–1919.* Rochester NY: John P. Smith Printing Co., 1919.

Sherwood, Elmer W. *Diary of a Rainbow Veteran: Written at the Front.* Terre Haute IN: Moore-Langen, 1929.

Stansbury, Henry D. *Maryland's 117th Trench Mortar Battery in the World War, 1917–1919.* Baltimore: John C. Lucas Printing, 1942.

Straub, Elmer Frank. *A Sergeant's Diary in the World War: The Diary of an Enlisted Member of the 150th Field Artillery (Forty-second [Rainbow] Division), October 27, 1917 to August 7, 1919.* Indianapolis: Indiana Historical Commission, 1923.

Taber, John H. *The Story of the 168th Infantry.* 2 vols. Iowa City: State Historical Society, 1925.

Tompkins, Raymond S. *The Story of the Rainbow Division.* New York: Boni & Liveright, 1919.

Triplet, William S. *A Youth in the Meuse-Argonne: A Memoir, 1917–1918.* Edited by Robert H. Ferrell. Columbia: University of Missouri Press, 2000.

Walker, George. *Venereal Disease in the American Expeditionary Forces.* Baltimore MD: Medical Standard Book Co., 1922.

Weaver, Frederic N. *The Story of F Company, 101st Regiment, U.S. Engineers: An Informal Narrative.* Boston: T. O. Metcalf Co., 1924.

Wilgus, William J. *Transporting the A.E.F. in Western Europe, 1917.* New York: Columbia University Press, 1931.

"With the Rainbow Division in France." *Therapeutic Digest* 14, no. 3 (July 1919): 7–14.

Young, Hugh. *Hugh Young: A Surgeon's Autobiography.* New York: Harcourt, Brace & Co., 1940.

Secondary Sources

Abrahamson, James L. *America Arms for a New Century: The Making of a Great Military Power*. New York: Free Press, 1981.

The Americans in the Great War. Vols. 1–3. Clermont-Ferrand, France: Michelin & Cie, 1920.

Baldwin, Fred Davis. "The American Enlisted Man in World War I." PhD diss., Princeton University, 1964.

Beaver, Daniel R. *Newton D. Beaver and the American War Effort, 1917–1919*. Lincoln: University of Nebraska Press, 1966.

Bond, P. S., and C. O. Sherrill. *America in the World War: A Summary of the Achievements of the Great Republic in the Conflict with Germany*. Menasha WI: George Banta, 1921.

Braim, Paul F. *The Test of Battle: The American Expeditionary Forces in the Meuse-Argonne Campaign*. Rev. ed. Shippensburg PA: White Mane, 1998.

Bridges, Clifton. "Through the Fire: A Study of the U.S. Army's 42nd Infantry Division in World War I." MA thesis, University of Nebraska–Lincoln, 1993.

Bristow, Nancy K. *Making Men Moral: Social Engineering During the Great War*. New York: New York University Press, 1996.

Bruce, Robert B. *A Fraternity of Arms: America and France in the Great War*. Lawrence: University Press of Kansas, 2003.

Burk, Kathleen. *Britain, America and the Sinews of War, 1914–1918*. Boston: Allen & Unwin, 1985.

Chambers, John Whiteclay, II. *To Raise an Army: The Draft Comes to America*. New York: Free Press, 1987.

Clark, George P., and Shirley E. Clark. "A New York Yank Narrates a Costly Victory at St. Mihiel." *Camaraderie* 8, no. 3 (November 2002): 4.

Clements, Kendrick A. *The Presidency of Woodrow Wilson*. Lawrence: University Press of Kansas, 1992.

Clifford, John Garry. *The Citizen Soldiers: The Plattsburg Training Camp Movement, 1913–1920*. Lexington: The University Press of Kentucky, 1972.

Coffman, Edward M. *The War to End All Wars: The American Military Experience in World War I*. Madison: University of Wisconsin Press, 1986.

Collins, Louis. *Minnesota in the World War*. Vol. 1. *History of 151st Field Artillery Rainbow Division*. Saint Paul: Minnesota War Records Commission, 1924.

Cooke, James J. *The Rainbow Division in the Great War, 1917–1919*. Westport CT: Praeger, 1994.

Cooke, Miriam, and Angela Woollacott, eds. *Gendering War Talk*. Princeton NJ: Princeton University Press, 1993.

Cooper, Jerry. *The Rise of the National Guard: The Evolution of the American Militia, 1865–1920*. Lincoln: University of Nebraska Press, 1997.

Cooper, John Milton, Jr. *Vanity of Power: American Isolationism and the First World War, 1914–1917*. Westport CT: Greenwood, 1969.

Corey, Herbert. "Cooties and Courage." *National Geographic Magazine* 33, no. 6 (June 1918): 495–509.

Cornebise, Alfred E., ed. *Doughboy Doggerel: Verse of the American Expeditionary Force, 1918–1919*. Athens: Ohio University Press, 1985.

Cowley, Robert, ed. *The Great War: Perspectives on the First World War*. New York: Random House, 2003.

Crowell, Benedict, and Robert Forrest Wilson. *How America Went to War—The Road to France, I and II: The Transportation of Troops and Military Supplies, 1917–1918*. New Haven CT: Yale University Press, 1921.

Deweerd, Harvey A. *President Wilson Fights His War: World War I and the American Intervention*. New York: Macmillan, 1968.

Dickinson, John. *The Building of an Army: A Detailed Account of Legislation, Administration and Opinion in the United States, 1915–1920*. New York: Century, 1922.

Eisenhower, John S. D. *Yanks: The Epic Story of the American Army in World War I*. New York: Free Press, 2001.

Ellis, John. *Eye-Deep in Hell: Trench Warfare in World War I*. Baltimore MD: Johns Hopkins University Press, 1976.

Farwell, Byron. *Over There: The United States in the Great War, 1917–1918*. New York: Norton, 1999.

Ferrell, Robert H. *Woodrow Wilson and World War I, 1917–1921*. New York: Harper & Row, 1985.

Finnegan, John Patrick. *Against the Specter of a Dragon: The Campaign for American Military Preparedness*. Westport CT: Greenwood Press, 1974.

Ford, Nancy Gentile. *Americans All! Foreign-born Soldiers in World War I*. College Station: Texas A & M University Press, 2001.

Fortescue, Granville. "Training the New Armies of Liberty." *National Geographic Magazine* 32, nos. 5–6 (November–December 1917): 421–37.

Freidel, Frank. *Over There: The Story of America's First Great Overseas Crusade*. New York: McGraw-Hill, 1990.

Frothingham, Thomas G. *American Reinforcement in the World War*. Garden City NY: Doubleday, Page & Co., 1927.

Garley, E. B., O. O. Ellis, and R. V. D. Magoffin. *American Guide Book to France and its Battlefields*. New York: MacMillan, 1920.

Genthe, Charles V. *American War Narratives, 1917–1918: A Study and Bibliography*. New York: Dale Lewis, 1969.

Gilbert, Martin. *The First World War: A Complete History*. New York: Henry Holt, 1994.

Goode, J. Roy. *The American Rainbow*. 1918.

Grayzel, Susan. *Women and the First World War*. New York: Longman, 2002.

Gregory, Ross. *The Origins of American Intervention in the First World War*. New York: Norton, 1971.

Hallas, James H. *Doughboy War: The American Expeditionary Force in World War II*. Boulder CO: Lynne Rienner, 2000.

———. *Squandered Victory: The American First Army at St. Mihiel*. Westport CT: Praeger, 1995.

Harries, Meirion, and Susie Harries. *The Last Days of Innocence: America at War, 1917–1918*. New York: Random House, 1997.

Herring, George C., Jr. "James Hay and the Preparedness Controversy, 1915–1916." *Journal of Southern History* 30, no. 4 (November 1964): 383–404.

Johnson, Douglas V., II, and Rolfe L. Hillman Jr. *Soissons 1918*. College Station: Texas A & M University Press, 1999.

Johnson, Thomas M. *Without Censor: New Light on Our Greatest World War Battles*. Indianapolis IN: Bobbs-Merrill, 1928.

Keegan, John. *The First World War*. New York: Alfred A. Knopf, 1998.

Keene, Jennifer D. *The United States in the First World War*. New York: Longman, 2000.

———. *Doughboys, the Great War, and the Remaking of America*. Baltimore MD: Johns Hopkins University Press, 2001.

Kennedy, David M. *Over There: The First World War and American Society*. New York: Oxford University Press, 1980.

Kindsvatter, Peter. *American Soldiers: Ground Combat in the World Wars, Korea, and Vietnam*. Lawrence: University Press of Kansas, 2003.

Koistinen, Paul A. C. *Mobilizing for Modern War: The Political Economy of American Warfare, 1865–1919*. Lawrence: University Press of Kansas, 1997.

Kutta, Timothy J. "The American Army in World War I." *Strategy and Tactics* (July–August 2003): 6–22.

Lancaster, Richard C. *Serving the U.S. Armed Forces, 1861–1986: The Story of the YMCA's Ministry to Military Personnel for 125 Years*. Schaumburg IL: Armed Services YMCA of the U.S.A., 1987.

Leed, Eric J. *No Man's Land: Combat and Identity in World War I*. New York: Cambridge University Press, 1979.

Linderman, Gerald F. *Embattled Courage: The Experience of Combat in the American Civil War*. New York: Free Press, 1987.

————. *The World Within War: America's Combat Experience in World War II*. Cambridge MA: Harvard University Press, 1997.

Link, Arthur S. *Woodrow Wilson and the Progressive Era, 1910–1917*. New York: Harper & Brothers, 1954.

————. *Woodrow Wilson: Revolution, War, and Peace*. Arlington Heights IL: Harlan Davidson, 1979.

Lovell, S. D. *The Presidential Election of 1916*. Carbondale: Southern Illinois University Press, 1980.

Lynn, John A. *The Bayonets of the Republic: Motivation and Tactics in the Army of Revolutionary France, 1791–94*. Chicago: University of Illinois Press, 1984.

MacDonald, Lyn. *1914–1918: Voices and Images of the Great War*. London: Michael Joseph, 1988.

Mackey, Frank J., and Marcus Wilson Jernegan. *Forward—March!*. Chicago: Disabled American Veterans of the World War, Department of Rehabilitation, 1935.

May, Ernest R. *The World War and American Isolation, 1914–1917*. Chicago IL: Quadrangle Books, 1959.

McClellan, Ewin. "The Aisne-Marne Offensive, Part 1." *Marine Corps Gazette* (March 1921): 68–84.

————. "The Aisne-Marne Offensive, Part 2." *Marine Corps Gazette* (June 1921): 188–227.

McPherson, James M. *For Cause and Comrades: Why Men Fought in the Civil War*. New York: Oxford University Press, 1997.

Mead, Gary. *The Doughboys: America and the First World War*. New York: Overlook, 2000.

Meigs, Mark. *Optimism at Armageddon: Voices of American Participants in the First World War*. New York: New York University Press, 1997.

Millett, Allan R., and Peter Maslowski. *For the Common Defense: A Military History of the United States of America*. New York: Free Press, 1994.

Millis, Walter. *Road to War: America, 1914–1917*. New York: Howard Fertig, 1970.

Nenninger, Timothy K. "American Military Effectiveness in the First World War." In *Military Effectiveness*, Vol. 1, *The First World War*, edited by Allan R. Millett and Williamson Murray, 116–56. Boston: Allen & Unwin, 1988.

————. "Tactical Dysfunction in the AEF, 1917–1918." *Military Affairs* 51, no. 4 (October 1987): 177–81.

Paschall, Rod. *The Defeat of Imperial Germany, 1917–1918*. Chapel Hill NC: Algonquin, 1989.

Pearlman, Michael. *To Make Democracy Safe for America: Patricians and Preparedness in the Progressive Era*. Urbana: University of Illinois Press, 1984.

Rainey, James W. "The Questionable Training of the AEF in World War I." *Parameters* (Winter 1992–93): 89–103.

————. "Ambivalent Warfare: The Tactical Doctrine of the AEF in World War I." *Parameters* (September 1983): 34–46.

Reilly, Henry J. *Americans All: The Rainbow at War.* Columbus OH: F. J. Heer Printing Co., 1936.

Robertson, Edgar E., and Victor J. West. *The Foreign Policy of Woodrow Wilson, 1913–1917.* New York: MacMillan, 1917.

Sadler, E. J., ed. *California Rainbow Memories: A Pictorial Review of the Activities of the 2nd Battalion, 117th Engineers During the World War.* Los Angeles: Smith-Barnes, 1925.

Schneider, Dorothy. *Into the Breach: American Women Overseas in World War I.* New York: Viking, 1991.

Seymour, Charles. *Woodrow Wilson and the World War.* New Haven CT: Yale University Press, 1921.

Shay, Michael E. *A Grateful Heart: The History of a World War I Field Hospital.* Westport CT: Greenwood, 2002.

Showalter, William Joseph. "America's New Soldier Cities." *National Geographic Magazine* 32, no. 5–6 (November–December 1917): 438–76.

Smith, Daniel M. "National Interest and American Intervention, 1917: An Historiographical Appraisal." *Journal of American History* 52, no. 1 (June 1965): 5–24.

Smythe, Donald. "Venereal Disease: The AEF's Experience." *Prologue: The Journal of the National Archives* 9, no. 2 (Summer 1977): 65–74.

————. "St. Mihiel: The Birth of an American Army." *Parameters* 13, no. 2 (June 1983): 47–57.

————. "The Pershing-March Conflict in World War I." *Parameters* 11, no. 4 (December 1981): 53–62.

Snead, David L., "South Carolina Engineers in the 42nd (Rainbow) Division in World War I." In *Proceedings of the South Carolina Historical Association,* edited by Stephen Lowe, 49–62. Columbia: South Carolina Historical Association, South Carolina Department of Archives and History, 2003.

Stallings, Laurence. *The Doughboys: The Story of the AEF, 1917–1918.* New York: Harper & Row, 1963.

Stokesbury, James L. "The Aisne-Marne Offensive." *American History Illustrated* 15, no. 4 (July 1980): 8–17.

Taft, William Howard, Frederick Harris, Frederic Houston Kent, William J. Newlin, eds. *Service with Fighting Men: An Account of the Work of the American Young Men's Christian Associations in the World War.* Vols. 1 and 2. New York: Association Press, 1924.

Thomas, Shipley. *The History of the A.E.F.* New York: George H. Doran, 1920.

Toland, John. *No Man's Land: 1918, The Last Year of the Great War.* Garden City NY: Doubleday, Page & Co., 1980.

Trask, David F. *The AEF and Coalition Warmaking, 1917–1918.* Lawrence: University Press of Kansas, 1993.

Tuchman, Barbara W. *The Zimmermann Telegram.* 1958. Reprint, New York: Ballentine, 1966.

Tucker, Spencer C. *The Great War, 1914–1918.* Bloomington: Indiana University Press, 1998.

Turner, L. C. F. *Origins of the First World War.* New York: Norton, 1970.

Vandiver, Frank E. *Black Jack: The Life and Times of John J. Pershing.* Vol. 2. College Station: Texas A & M University Press, 1977.

Victory, James. "Soldier Making: The Forces That Shaped the Infantry Training of White Soldiers in the United States Army in World War I," PhD diss., Kansas State University, 1990.

Viereck, George Sylvester, ed. *As They Saw Us: Foch, Ludendorff, and Other Leaders Write Our War History.* Garden City NY: Doubleday, Doran & Co., 1929.

Ward, Robert D. "The Origin and Activities of the National Security League, 1914–1919." *Mississippi Valley Historical Review* 47, no. 1 (June 1960): 51–65.

Weik, Laura Stoddard. *"One Hundred Years": History of Morris CT, 1859–1959.* Morris CT: Morris Centennial Committee, 1959.

Wolf, Walter B. *A Brief History of the Rainbow Division.* New York: Rand, McNally, 1919.

Zeiger, Susan. *In Uncle Sam's Service: Women Workers with the American Expeditionary Force, 1917–1919.* Ithaca NY: Cornell University Press, 1999.

Ziegler, Robert H. *America's Great War: World War I and the American Experience.* Lanham MD: Rowman & Littlefield, 2000.

Soldiers as Citizens
Former German Officers in the
Federal Republic of Germany, 1945–1955
Jay Lockenour

Army and Empire
British Soldiers on the
American Frontier, 1758–1775
Michael N. McConnell

The Militarization of Culture in the
Dominican Republic, from the Captains
General to General Trujillo
Valentina Peguero

Arabs at War
Military Effectiveness, 1948–1991
Kenneth M. Pollack

The Politics of Air Power
From Confrontation to Cooperation in
Army Aviation Civil-Military Relations
Rondall R. Rice

The Grand Illusion
The Prussianization of the Chilean Army
William F. Sater and Holger H. Herwig

The Paraguayan War: Volume 1,
Causes and Early Conduct
Thomas L. Whigham

The Challenge of Change
Military Institutions and New Realities, 1918–1941
Edited by Harold R. Winton and David R. Mets

CPSIA information can be obtained at www.ICGtesting.com
Printed in the USA
LVOW07s0639211014

409701LV00001B/6/P